LIFE
ON THE
LINE

When you are prepared to
give up everything for God,
He will show up in your life
in ways you cannot imagine!

International evangelists Dr Desmond and Roslynn Sinclair live their lives to the full, not scared of dying for what they believe and for the miracle-working God they serve.

At the age of eleven a gun was pointed to Des's head because he dared to talk about Jesus to a drug-crazed gangster, but the trigger misfired three times. He has been hijacked, imprisoned, tortured, beaten and left for dead, yet God supernaturally intervened to preserve his life.

Today he and his wife Ros travel the world, challenging the body of Christ to overcome their fears and stand unwaveringly in their faith in God. They are a couple who have laid everything they have on the line for God, and He has taken their lives and made them a lifeline to the nations.

> *Seldom has a book gripped my attention as much as this one!*
>
> Raymond Fuchs, South African businessman

> *I've read thousands of books, but nothing moved me more powerfully. You can't afford to miss this life-changing book.*
>
> Prof. J. Potgieter,
> Trinity/Therapon Universities, USA

> Life on the Line *held me riveted and amazed at the goodness and love of our miracle-working God. I have heard these stories from the life of Des and Ros Sinclair before, but Al Gibson has brought them alive in an amazing way... I believe* Life on the Line *will bring multitudes into the Kingdom.*
>
> Linda Shutte,
> Mondeor Baptist Church Prison Ministry,
> South Africa

About the Author

Christian journalist Al Gibson has a passion to report on what God is doing in the world today through His servants in different countries – men and women of God who so obviously belong in Hebrews 11's 'Hall of Faith'. These are people 'who through faith subdued kingdoms, worked righteousness, obtained promises, stopped the mouths of lions, quenched the violence of fire, escaped the edge of the sword, out of weakness were made strong' (Hebrews 11:33–34).

Al works for GOD TV (www.god.tv) as central communications officer for the global television network and is privileged to serve Rory and Wendy Alec's awesome vision of winning one billion souls for the Kingdom of God.

LIFE
ON THE
LINE

*When you put your life on the line for God,
it will become a lifeline for others*

The extraordinary life and ministry of Des and Ros Sinclair as told to Al Gibson

They loved not their lives unto the death.
Revelation 12:11, KJV

MONARCH
BOOKS

Oxford, UK & Grand Rapids, Michigan, USA

First published in the UK in 2009 by Monarch Books
(a publishing imprint of Lion Hudson plc),
Wilkinson House, Jordan Hill Road, Oxford OX2 8DR.
Tel: +44 (0)1865 302750 Fax: +44 (0)1865 302757
Email: monarch@lionhudson.com
www.lionhudson.com

ISBN: 978-1-85424-900-5 (UK)
ISBN: 978-0-8254-6304-4 (USA)

Distributed by:
UK: Marston Book Services Ltd, PO Box 269, Abingdon, Oxon OX14 4YN;
USA: Kregel Publications, PO Box 2607, Grand Rapids, Michigan 49501

British Library Cataloguing Data
A catalogue record for this book is available from the British Library.

Printed and bound in England by CPI Cox & Wyman.

Contents

A Message to Our Readers   9

Acknowledgements   11

Foreword by Peter Whitcombe   13

1. The Sentence is Death! – *West Africa*   17

2. If You Come Back, I'll Kill You! – *New Zealand*   33

3. The God Who Answers with Fire – *Ghana*   45

4. A Bright Light in the Darkness – *South Africa*   56

5. Is This What Heaven is Like? – *Heaven (Part 1)*   69

6. What Will You Die For? – *Ghana*   83

7. I'm a Dead Man! – *Ghana*   94

8. Pressing on Towards the Mark – *Australia*   104

9. Dying is Easy, Living is the Challenge
   – *Heaven (Part 2)*   120

10. You'd Better Talk... or Die! – *Angola/South Africa*   131

11. Back to the Rubbish Dump – *Kenya*   141

12. There is a Better Way – *South Africa*   154

13. A Fate Worse than Death – *South Africa/Mozambique* 168

14. The Blood of the Martyrs Cries Out – *Heaven (Part 3)*
    and Hell   176

15. You Will Stand Before Kings – *South America*   188

16. Behold, I Give You Power – *Zimbabwe/Nigeria*   201

17. God's Grace is Sufficient – *South Africa*   214

18. Look Who is Cheering Us On – *Heaven (Part 4)*   222

19. Holding Out the Word of Life – *Life Evangelism International*   230

20. You are Immortal Until God's Will for Your Life is Complete – *Conclusion*   238

Appendix 1: About Life Evangelism International   249

Appendix 2: Ministry Endorsements   251

A Message to Our Readers

FROM DES AND ROS SINCLAIR

Dear Reader

We want to give praise and honour to God for what He has done in our lives and thank Him for all that He has called us to do as a couple – for all the many times He has delivered us from impossible situations and all the miracles He has done through the ministry of Life Evangelism International.

Our one concern about publishing this book is that readers may get the wrong impression that we are something special or have a unique hotline to God – or that the experiences you will read about are daily occurrences in our lives.

Please understand that we are just ordinary people sold out to an extraordinary God – simply walking by faith that we will accurately hear the voice of the Holy Spirit, just like any other believer. Also know that the experiences shared here did not take place all at once, which is why this is a book, not a magazine article or news report!

There is so much the Lord has done over the past twenty years in our ministry for which we are enormously grateful, and we share these things, not to boast in ourselves, but to chronicle how faithful our God is and what a privilege it is to serve Him.

We also want to encourage you concerning your own life and to challenge you to believe God for the miraculous in the impossible situations you face. For the Lord is not a respecter of persons, and what He has done for us, He can and will do for you, as you trust Him.

Des and Ros

Acknowledgments

We would like to thank everyone who has contributed to the publication of this book, in whatever way, as well as to acknowledge the following people who have made a significant impact on our lives.

In memory of Dr Sir Sebastian Malamb and Dr Marvin Wolford

We fondly remember evangelist Sebastian Malamb as a good friend who burned with an incredible passion for souls and was always prepared to put his life on the line as a freedom fighter for Jesus. He was a wonderful example to us, inspiring us in our evangelistic call, and we are so grateful to the Lord that he was our friend.

We also remember Dr Marvin Wolford for his great wisdom in ministry, his father's heart towards all men, his compassion, and for being someone who truly walked with God, constantly putting his life on the line for Jesus.

Thank you to the following dear friends

Pastor Peter and Sue Whitcombe: You are a couple who are not ashamed of the Gospel, and you boldly live out what you believe. Thank you for your apostolic impartation into our lives while we served in your church, and for believing in us as a couple.

Sean and Gena Mullin: Thank you for all your support during a very trying time, and for your unconditional love by taking us into your home, when we would otherwise have found ourselves homeless on the streets of Johannesburg. We so appreciate everything you did for us.

Raymond and Renate Fuchs: Thank you for your confidence in our ministry and for being such solid pillars of support, always there for us, with a passion to see God's plan for our lives come to pass.

Mike and Marit Sutton: Thank you for your love and support over the years and for believing in the call of God on our lives. We love and appreciate you.

May the Lord bless you and your families and ministries richly.

Foreword

When I read *Life on the Line*, the amazing story of what God has done and is doing through Des and Ros Sinclair, I was reminded of a comment often heard in Church circles in recent years, which states that the Church needs to return to the Book of the Acts of the Apostles (which is really the Acts of the Holy Spirit through the Apostles).

The inference in this statement is that the Church needs to walk again in the demonstration and power of the Holy Spirit as recorded in the Book of Acts. In reading *Life on the Line*, you will see that the Sinclairs are one couple who are walking in that kind of demonstration and power of the Holy Spirit, and you will be encouraged and challenged by what God can do through everyday people like them.

Jesus declares in Mark 16:17–18 (Amplified):

> *And these attesting signs will accompany those who believe: in My name they will drive out demons; they will speak in new languages; they will pick up serpents; and [even] if they drink anything deadly, it will not hurt them; they will lay their hands on the sick, and they will get well.*

This promise that Jesus gives is not just to pastors and elders and visiting evangelists but to believers – that is, to those who believe. Jesus says that 'attesting signs' (or confirming signs) will accompany the life and the ministry of believers. He says also in John 14:12, 'Most assuredly, I say to you, he who believes in Me, the works that I do he will do also; and greater works than these he will do, because I go to My Father.'

In Matthew 24:14 Jesus declares: 'And this Gospel of the Kingdom will be preached in all the world as a witness to all the nations, and then the end will come.'

We know from Scripture that the Good News of the Kingdom is a superior authority, and that power has come through Christ, and that the Kingdom of God is within us, and that the power and the authority of that Kingdom has been conferred to us (Matthew 16:18–19; Luke 12:32; 22:29).

As ambassadors of Christ, we have been given the responsibility to do what Jesus did and to do what the disciples did, which is to manifest the reality of the Kingdom of God in undoing the works of the devil in every life and in every place under the dominion of the devil.

We are called to represent (literally re-present) the fullness of the life and the ministry of Jesus, to impact lives and cities and nations with the Gospel of the Kingdom, to heal the sick, raise the dead, cast out demons and cleanse the lepers (that is, the unsaved – those whose lives are blighted by sin).

Jesus makes a powerful statement in John 10:37–38: 'If I do not do the works of My Father, do not believe Me; but if I do, though you do not believe Me, believe the works, that you may know and believe that the Father is in Me, and I in Him.'

In effect He is saying, 'Do not believe that I am who I say I am on the basis of what the prophets of old have said, or on the basis of what John the Baptist said or on the basis of My virgin birth. Do not believe Me because of the words that I speak or on the basis of My teaching. Instead, believe on the basis of the works that I do, believe on the basis of the miracles, because they testify of Me and they confirm My words.'

As you read this exciting and powerful book, you will see that Des and Ros Sinclair are a couple who not only believe what Jesus says, but they also live it! They are 'everyday' people, living the Book of Acts every day! They are a couple who can stand and declare as Jesus did (and as the Church must become able to do today), 'Don't simply believe what we say about Jesus, believe that He is the Son of God and the Saviour by the works that we do in His name.'

The Sinclairs are a living testimony that Jesus is the same yesterday, today and forever, and that just as He turned the known world the right side up in a very short period of time (as recorded in the Book of Acts) through a group of everyday people, so too today, He can impact our world through everyday people. Jesus is seeking those who will live like Des and Ros Sinclair, who will live wholeheartedly for Him, who are dead to their own desires and their own plans and purposes, but are alive to Christ.

Wherever Jesus finds those who will believe, who will trust and who will obey wholeheartedly as the Sinclairs have done and continue to do, then He will move in power through them, and the Gospel of the Kingdom will be manifested and demonstrated in all the earth as a witness.

Wherever Jesus finds sold-out sons and daughters like Des and Ros, there will be attesting signs accompanying such people, and the lives of others will be powerfully changed, and towns and cites and nations will be impacted for Christ.

As you read *Life on the Line*, allow the Holy Spirit to inspire you to live wholeheartedly for the Lord and to challenge you, that you too can make a difference wherever you are. Your experiences may not be as 'challenging' as Des's and Ros's, and you may not preach to multitudes in crusades, but if you are a believer, then a life walking in the authority and the power of God, with signs accompanying you as you live and minister, is God's plan and purpose for you.

Heaven is recording the Acts of the Holy Spirit today, not just through Apostles, Prophets, Pastors and Teachers, but through everyday people who will live for Jesus and who will trust Him and obey Him.

Peter Whitcombe,
Senior Pastor, Jesus First, Auckland, New Zealand

Chapter 1

The Sentence is Death!

'You have blasphemed Allah. Now you must die!'

'If you renounce Jesus Christ your life will be spared,' the Muslim judge told the young evangelist, spitting out the words with an air of superiority, as if he was making an offer that could not be refused.

Even as the words cut deep into Des Sinclair's soul, he knew this was not even an option. He had long since come to know the joy of being persecuted for the cause of Christ. Even so, he was desperately seeking God's wisdom in this present crisis. Was this really the end of the road for him, or did the Lord have other plans?

It was 1997. He had been preaching in Burkina Faso in West Africa, when he had been abducted and smuggled across the border into Mali – a country known for its devotion to radical Islam. Just a few hours before he had been proclaiming freedom and deliverance in Jesus; now he was in chains before a hostile Muslim court.

After a series of outstanding crusades in Accra, Ghana, Des had been invited to minister in Burkina Faso, where he preached in local churches in the capital, Ouagadougou. Then came the request which would change everything: 'We believe the Lord wants you to help us to do a mass Gospel crusade right near the border of Mali!'

17

God moved sovereignly on the first night. A crowd of 15,000 had gathered and a third of the people gave their lives to the Lord. Des was overjoyed as he received confirmation that 5,000 people had registered their decisions to follow Christ.

Nothing could dampen his spirits, not even a warning from the pastors from Burkina Faso, who had told Des that radical Muslims from Mali had abducted preachers in the past and taken them to prisons across the border, and that he should be very careful.

'That could never happen to me,' Des had thought to himself at the time. 'God would never allow that. I am covered by the blood of Jesus.' The thought of being taken captive was something quite foreign to his Western way of thinking, and he quickly put it out of his mind.

The crowd was even bigger on the second night, as more and more people, including many Muslims, gathered to witness the healing power of God at work. Des was so excited as he began to preach the Gospel. Blind eyes started to open and the Lord began to reveal His glory in an incredible way.

Later that night Des was woken up with a start as God began to speak to him as he lay in bed at the pastor's home where he was staying. It wasn't an audible voice, but Des knew very clearly that the Lord had spoken, though it was not something he wanted to hear: 'I am with you. Do not fear, but they are coming to get you and they will take you.'

Then at about half past one in the morning there was a great commotion outside the house, as Des was woken up again, this time by the sound of gunshots. He jumped out of bed and ran to the window, where he was shocked to see the bodies of his host and his wife lying dead in the yard.

'Lord, is this a vision or is this for real?' Des questioned, now wide awake but battling to come to terms with the horror of what was going on around him.

This dear couple had tragically lost their lives while trying to protect Des and were now lying motionless in the African dust. Then Des heard more shots being fired as another pastor who had been staying in the house met his untimely death.

Then four armed men dressed like nomads from the desert grabbed Des violently and pushed him, prodding him with the barrels of their guns into a waiting vehicle.

'They are going to kill me, Lord,' Des whispered to God in prayer. 'They have killed everyone else and they are going to kill me now. Lord, if it's my time, take me. Thank You for forgiving my sins and for Your blood, which cleanses me from all unrighteousness.'

'I told you they were coming to get you. Do not fear – I am with you,' came the still, small voice within. And all of a sudden a great peace came over Des and he knew that God had everything under control.

'Where are you taking me?' Des cried out to the men, but they were shouting and screaming in a foreign language and he could not understand a word they were saying. 'Lord, if You are with me, then all is well,' he said under his breath, not trying to resist or get away.

The Muslim henchmen bribed the border guards to allow them through the border post without passports, and they continued to travel for many hours until they reached a high-security prison complex. Here Des's wrists and ankles were chained and he was shoved into a filthy old cell and chained to the floor.

Sitting there on the bare concrete, hardly able to move, it began to dawn on Des that his captors wanted to make a public spectacle of him for converting Muslims to Christianity.

'Lord, why am I here and what is going to happen to me?' Des cried out to God.

The Lord said, 'I brought you here as a testimony that I am the risen Lord, and that I will deliver My own from the hand of the enemy. Trust Me.'

Despite his chains, Des knew that God was with him, and he made a conscious decision to rejoice in the Lord. 'Lord, You are with me, and if this is my last day here on earth, I am going to praise You, because death has no power over me,' he boldly proclaimed. 'And even if I am going to stay in jail for the rest of my life, I know there is a reason why I am here, and I will preach the Gospel. Even if there is only one man in this jail who will receive Christ as Saviour, then it will all be worth it. For You may raise up that one man to do greater things than I could ever do.'

It was almost impossible to sleep with the chains cutting into his flesh, but Des had an assurance that God was in control. 'The steps of a righteous man are ordered from above,' he thought. 'I am not going to allow myself to despair. God has allowed this to happen for His glory. I am in God's hands.'

At that moment Des remembered the tiny Bible hidden in his clothing, as was his habit when ministering in West Africa, and was overjoyed to be able to read the Scriptures. Fortunately he had not been subjected to a body search and was now able to build himself up in the Word, praising the Lord and thanking Him, in spite of his desperate circumstances.

The next morning, Des was taken to appear before a renegade Islamic tribunal, where he found himself in front of several people, including a vicious-looking Muslim judge, whose hatred was tangible.

'You have been preaching this man Jesus and have

been misleading our people,' shouted the judge in broken English, as many angry faces looked on in contempt.

'How could I have misled your people?' Des tried to reply quietly. 'I have never been to your country. It is you who have brought me here. I never...'

'S-i-l-e-n-c-e!' said the judge, not wanting to hear any more. 'You must renounce this Jesus and sign a declaration saying He is not God. You have been telling our people lies. Jesus Christ is dead.'

Then one by one, many witnesses were called, to give some semblance of a 'fair' trial, each explaining in detail to the court what they had heard Des preaching. 'He told us that Jesus is the risen Lord... the only Son of God...' said one man, furiously waving his finger.

'Will you stop doing this?' asked the judge. 'If you renounce Jesus Christ you will not receive the death penalty. Your life will be spared, but you will still have to serve a prison sentence of thirty years.'

'I will never renounce Jesus Christ, because He is the truth,' replied Des. 'I would rather be killed by you than let Him down.'

There was a hushed silence in the court room, which quickly broke into an angry outburst as the men of the tribunal conferred amongst themselves.

Then one the officers of the court delivered the ominous verdict: 'You have been tried and found guilty of breaking the laws of Mali. You have blasphemed Allah and the prophet Mohammed, and the sentence is death. You will be executed by a firing squad tomorrow morning at seven o'clock.'

At that, armed guards grabbed Des and shoved him on the back of an old pick-up truck and took him back to prison. But this time he was taken to the execution section, where he was locked up in a cell with two other inmates, also on 'death row'.

With just twelve hours to live, Des began to pray: 'Lord, is my time up? Am I coming home? Is this where I am going to end up?' Many different questions began to flood through his mind as he battled to come to terms with this hopeless situation.

But there were two other men in the cell with him who had also been sentenced to death, and Des knew they were facing a hellish eternity. 'Lord, if I am going home, these men are going to die as well, and I have to try to communicate with them. Lord, I want to share the Gospel with them and at least try to save them from eternal death.'

One of the men was from Ghana and spoke English well, while the other could only speak French. 'Where do you stand with Jesus?' Des asked the Ghanaian. 'Do you have an assurance that when you leave this earth, you are going to live with the Lord forever? Is Jesus your Lord and Saviour, or are you going to be separated from Him and tormented in hell? Choose this day who you will serve,' he said, quoting from Deuteronomy 30:19. 'Choose life, choose Jesus – because life only comes through accepting Him as your Saviour. You are not going to get another chance to hear this. You have to make a decision now to repent of your sins. Tomorrow you will be dead.'

Tears began to stream from the man's eyes as he listened intently. 'I am such a bad person,' he said. 'I have heard of Jesus before. I went to church as a young man growing up in Kumasi, but I have always done my own thing. But now I am a criminal and my life is going to be taken from me...' He was so scared, he was shaking.

'I know that when I stand before God, He will reject me. I am not worthy and He won't receive me.' He started to talk about all the offences he had committed in his life. Des began to minister to him, and tell him how much Jesus wanted to reach out to him in his despair.

'What is your name?' Des asked.

'Tecoli!'

'Well, Tecoli, it does not matter what you have done – all that matters is where you are going. Jesus loves you and God has brought me here to this prison, and He has allowed me to be chained beside you, so that I can tell you this. Choose life, repent from your sins and ask Jesus to forgive you. Then we can thank the Lord, and you will have the assurance of eternal life.'

Des opened his little Bible once again and began to share more from the Scriptures, assuring Tecoli that Jesus had not come to condemn him but to release him from his sin and guilt. Des read these verses:

> *For God so loved the world that He gave His only begotten Son, that whoever believes in Him should not perish but have everlasting life. For God did not send His Son into the world to condemn the world, but that the world through Him might be saved.*
>
> *He who believes in Him is not condemned; but he who does not believe is condemned already, because he has not believed in the name of the only begotten Son of God.*
>
> John 3:16–18

With tears in his eyes, the Ghanaian prayed the sinner's prayer and gave his heart to the Lord. 'Let's praise the Lord,' Des said. 'Do you remember any songs from your Sunday School days?' And so they began to worship the Lord together and thank Him.

But while they sang such timeless classics as 'Yes, Jesus Loves Me', the third man in the cell looked on with seasoned indifference.

'Do you know any French?' Des asked. 'We need to try to reach out to our friend here. He's also going to be executed tomorrow.'

'I can speak a little bit of French,' Tecoli replied, and so through some makeshift interpreting, Des was able to communicate with the man from the Ivory Coast, a former French colony.

But his heart was hard towards the Gospel. 'I don't believe in Jesus,' he said. 'If God was alive He would not have allowed me to come to this place. My life has been so difficult. God is out to destroy me and it is better for me to die.'

Des pleaded with him for hours: 'That does not have to be your destiny. Tomorrow you are going to live forever or die forever – it's your choice.'

And although he refused to respond to Jesus, he did make one request. 'Tomorrow, when you stand before your God, remember me.'

Tears filled Des's eyes as he prayed for the man's heart to be opened. 'Lord, please reveal yourself to Him so that He can stand before you without judgment.' And again he tried to reach out to the man, but he refused to converse further.

But right there in that prison cell, as Des and his new-found brother in Christ continued to sing and read the Word, the presence of the Lord started to fall. You could see the Holy Spirit breathing all over the new convert, almost as if there was an orange-red glaze around his head.

The man from the Ivory Coast's eyes were popping out of his head in amazement, but for the two believers, nothing mattered. It was like God had come down to them in that cell, and they were overwhelmed by His presence.

'There is something like fire that is resting over you,' said the man from the Ivory Coast in French. 'What is it?'

'It is the Holy Spirit,' Des replied, with Tecoli interpreting. 'It is God's promise to the believer that the Holy Spirit will descend upon us,' he explained, quoting the book of Acts, which says: 'But you shall receive power when the Holy Spirit has come upon you; and you shall be witnesses to Me in Jerusalem, and in all Judea and Samaria, and to the end of the earth' (Acts 1:8).

'This is the witness,' continued Des. 'It is the baptism of the Holy Spirit. Something like tongues of fire will descend upon us, and that is what is happening here. The Spirit of God is upon us.'

Then all of a sudden, through the thick steel bars, a very tall man dressed in white could be seen walking up the long, narrow corridor towards them. He bypassed the first set of Muslim guards, and continued walking towards the two armed guards just outside the cell.

'Who is this?' Des thought. 'He doesn't look like he's from Mali. I wonder if he is an interpreter they have called to talk to me?'

The guards completely ignored the tall man, as he somehow managed to push the gate open and came straight into the cell.

Des thought he was dreaming – he couldn't believe what was happening. 'Do you see what I see?' he asked Tecoli in a whisper.

'I see what you see!'

'Tell me, what do you see?'

'I see a man who just pushed the prison gate open. He's tall, he's big and he glows like the sun!'

'Get up and follow me!' commanded the tall man with great authority. 'God has heard your cry and He has not finished with your life yet.'

'How can we get up?' Des answered. 'We're chained to the floor!'

'Put your hands up,' replied the tall man, looking at the chains, and they immediately broke and fell off Des and the Ghanaian. But the man from the Ivory Coast remained chained to the ground. He also tried to get up, but he could not.

'Remember me!' he yelled in French.

'What about him?' Des asked. 'We can't leave him here – he's going to die tomorrow.'

'It is finished,' came the reply. 'You spoke to him, you gave him the opportunity of grace. But he rejected it, so I can do nothing more for him. Follow me.'

And so the three men walked straight out of the cell. The guards did not even notice. Des still thought he was dreaming as the prison gates opened one after another and they continued walking.

'Where are you taking us? Where are we going?' he asked. 'How are we going to get out of here? They are going to come and kill us.'

'Follow me!' replied the tall man.

Des was amazed. Before he knew it, they had walked right out of the prison. Astounded, he kept following his rescuer for about an hour and ten minutes, until they arrived in a particular township, where they stopped at a particular door. Des looked up at the man dressed in white. He was about seven feet tall and looked like an American football player with huge shoulders.

It was a double-storey building and Des could hear a noise coming from the second floor. It sounded like chanting. It was about half past three and they could see the faint hint of a new day dawning on the horizon.

'Knock on the door,' their rescuer instructed. 'These people have been praying for you, that God would deliver you. God has spoken to them and told them how to get you to the border.

'Knock on the door – they are expecting you and have everything prepared. They will feed you and get you to the border without being caught. Then I will come and meet up with you again.'

'Knock on the door, man,' Des said to Tecoli, 'I am trying to keep this guy here. We can't let him leave us here.'

Then all of a sudden a young girl came running down the stairs and opened the top part of the door to poke her head out. Immediately she slammed it shut and went running back up the stairs.

The three men in the doorway could hear a great commotion as more people came to the door and flung it open. 'Quick – come in!' said a man in broken English, moving his hands in great excitement.

Des turned to greet him, and when he looked back, his tall rescuer was nowhere to be seen. His new host was trying to push him up the stairs as quickly as possible, along with his new friend from Ghana.

'Who are you?' Des enquired. 'Are you Muslims?'

'No, we are Christians, and we have been praying for you all night. We know what has happened and God told us He would deliver you.'

'Who was that man in white?' Des asked, as the reality of the situation dawned upon him.

'We don't know who he is. All we can think is that the Lord sent an angel to get you out of prison. There is no way you could have done that yourself.'

'He said you would take us to the border.'

'That's right. While we were praying, God revealed to us that you were coming, and everything is ready. Have some breakfast quickly – we need to leave right away! We need to get you out of here before daylight.'

After they had something to eat, Des and Tecoli were hastily hidden under blankets in the back of an old Toyota Landcruiser, and they were soon on their way to the border, covered by baskets filled with food and grain.

It was getting light very quickly, and all of a sudden the vehicle came to an abrupt stop. 'You must get out now!' came the urgent instruction from the driver as Des's eyes adjusted to the early morning sun.

As he looked around, he could see a primitive border post ahead of him. 'What are we going to do now?' he said to Tecoli. 'We have no passports. How are we going to get across the border?'

'We have done what God told us to do,' said the driver. 'He showed us the route to take to get you here, and He will take you where He wants you to go.'

'God will help us get across the border into Burkina Faso?' Des asked as he surveyed the remote crossing, with its high fences and armed guards.

'God will get you to the place where he wants you to go,' was the firm answer.

Des started to pray: 'Lord, You have got us this far. What are You going to do now?'

The next minute the same man who had rescued them from prison came walking towards them. Des now realized that he must be an angel sent from heaven.

'How are we going to get across the border with no passports?' he asked respectfully. 'The authorities will arrest us and they will arrest you too!' Then Des thought,

Don't be stupid! How can they arrest him? He's an angel!'

The instruction was the same as before: 'Follow me!'

Maybe we could try to dig under the fence further up, Des thought. It would be so much better if they tried to get across where they could not be seen. But instead they headed directly towards the border crossing, walking straight past the guards, pushing the gates open without being noticed.

All of a sudden, Des felt a strong, warm breeze and heard the sound of a whirlwind. It was almost as if God was breathing upon them, and the next minute they were walking through an African marketplace.

'Where are we?' Des asked the Ghanaian.

'We are in my home town, Kumasi!'

'But we can't be in Ghana. Kumasi is a thousand miles away!' Des said, realizing that was exactly where they were as he began to recognize the familiar surroundings of Kumasi's marketplace, where he had preached so many times before.

'What do we do now?' Des asked the man in white.

'Go to the King of Ghana. You know him from past crusades, and he will arrange for you to leave the country without any problems.'

It was time for Des and his new convert to go their separate ways. 'God has shown us incredible favour,' he said to Tecoli in parting. 'Go now and tell everybody what He has done.'

Des headed straight for the King's palace. How could he explain this whole story to him?

A London-trained lawyer, King Otumfuo Nana Opoku Ware II was more commonly known as 'the Asantehene' – the leader of the Ashanti people of Ghana. He had become the eighteenth King of Ashanti in 1970 and was nearing the end of his reign (he died in February 1999). How opportune of God to bring Des into this great leader's life just before he died.

'God is with you,' said King Otumfuo, 'and I will help you.'

Within days Des was on a plane flying back to South Africa. True to his word, King Otumfuo had helped him retrieve his passport, air-ticket and belongings from Burkina Faso, and he was now heading home.

Once again he had miraculously escaped death. The Lord had spared him to tell this extraordinary story of how God can intervene in the affairs of man, when we are truly sold out to Him and the cause of the Gospel.

Unbelievable, some may say... I wonder what the Apostle Peter would have thought of this story? Or how about the young girl, Rhoda, who was so dumbfounded by his supernatural release that she closed the door in his face – what would she have thought of it?

Or Paul and Silas, whose chains broke open as they sang songs of praise to the Lord at midnight? Or Phillip and the Ethiopian eunuch, who were divinely transported from one place to another?

Clearly, there are distinct biblical parallels. But none so profound as the way Jesus ministered to the two criminals on crosses beside Him. The one accepted the Lord, and Jesus assured him that he would immediately join Him in Paradise. The other rejected the Lord and, tragically, like the French-speaking man from the Ivory Coast, went to a lost eternity.

Des Sinclair will be the first to tell you that he is nothing special. What God has done for him, He can do for you. But there is a price to pay: total devotion to the Lord Jesus and a passion for the lost.

Peter freed from prison (Acts 12:5–17)

Peter was therefore kept in prison, but constant prayer was offered to God for him by the church. And when Herod was about to bring him out, that night Peter was sleeping, bound with two chains between two soldiers; and the guards before the door were keeping the prison.

Now behold, an angel of the Lord stood by him, and a light shone in the prison; and he struck Peter on the side and raised him up, saying, 'Arise quickly!' And his chains fell off his hands. Then the angel said to him, 'Gird yourself and tie on your sandals'; and so he did. And he said to him, 'Put on your garment and follow me.'

So he went out and followed him, and did not know that what was done by the angel was real, but thought he was seeing a vision. When they were past the first and the second guard posts, they came to the iron gate that leads to the city, which opened to them of its own accord; and they went out and went down one street, and immediately the angel departed from him.

And when Peter had come to himself, he said, 'Now I know for certain that the Lord has sent His angel, and has delivered me from the hand of Herod and from all the expectation of the Jewish people.' So, when he had considered this, he came to the house of Mary, the mother of John whose surname was Mark, where many were gathered together praying.

And as Peter knocked at the door of the gate, a girl named Rhoda came to answer. When she recognized Peter's voice, because of her gladness she did not open the gate, but ran in and announced that Peter stood before the gate. But they said to her, 'You are beside yourself!' Yet she kept insisting that it was so. So they said, 'It is his angel.'

Now Peter continued knocking; and when they opened the door and saw him, they were astonished. But motioning to them with his hand to keep silent, he declared to them how the Lord had brought him out of the prison. And he said, 'Go, tell these things to James and to the brethren.' And he departed and went to another place.

Two criminals hang on crosses alongside Jesus (Luke 23:39–43)

Then one of the criminals who were hanged blasphemed Him, saying, 'If You are the Christ, save Yourself and us.' But the other, answering, rebuked him, saying, 'Do you not even fear God, seeing you are under the same condemnation? And we indeed justly, for we receive the due reward of our deeds; but this Man has done nothing wrong.' Then he said to Jesus, 'Lord, remember me when You come into Your kingdom.' And Jesus said to him, 'Assuredly, I say to you, today you will be with Me in Paradise.'

Chapter 2

If You Come Back, I'll Kill You!

NEW ZEALAND

'Get out! You're no son of mine! And if you ever come back here, I'll kill you!'

'You leave my mother alone!' the young boy cried out as he tried to stop the man from lashing out at the woman he adored. The fighting had been going on for days and he could no longer stand by and witness such abuse.

At the tender age of eleven he was not really old enough to do much, but he still had an overwhelming urge to protect the women in his life – his mother and two sisters.

Des's dad was angry again and, as usual, was giving his mother and sisters a hard time. His father was very intolerant about anything to do with God and was often verbally abusive. His mother was a believer in the Lord, but Christianity was not encouraged in the home in any way, and she and her two daughters were often at the receiving end of much aggression. Intimidated and fearful, all they could do was toe the line and wait for the anger to subside.

Somehow Des seemed to have escaped the abuse, up until now, but that was all about to change. 'Don't you dare tell me what to do! You keep out of this, or I'll give you the hiding of your life!' his father shouted at the top of his voice.

'You can't speak to my mother like that, Dad!' Des replied in defence. This only made matters worse, and something triggered in his dad that would leave Des out on the street. Within a few minutes, his father had gone into his room, packed his clothes into a small suitcase and thrown him out the front door.

'You're not welcome here any more!' he shouted. 'You are no longer any part of this family. You have dared to stand against me, so now you must fend for yourself. *Get out!* You're no son of mine, and if you ever come back here, I'll kill you!'

Des was stunned, but he realized there was nothing he could do to make his father see reason. His first reaction was to knock on neighbours' doors – not that the family had many friends, due to all the inhouse fighting. But it soon became clear that the community did not want to know about his problems.

'What happened?' was the question Des was faced with, time and time again, as the list of doors he could knock on quickly diminished.

'My dad's booted me out! Please can I stay over with you tonight?' he pleaded.

'Definitely not!' came the reply, again and again, as fear filled the eyes of the neighbours. Go now, before he sees you with us.'

And so Des Sinclair's abrupt leap to adulthood began. Not yet a teenager, he was forced to look after himself on the streets. As darkness began to descend on the small town of Levin, near Wellington on New Zealand's North Island, the reality of having no home and no bed began to weigh heavily on the young lad's shoulders as he wandered along the bare pavements aimlessly.

'Where to now?' he thought, as he came upon a

rubbish dump on the wrong side of town. At least there were people there, scratching around looking for whatever discarded 'treasure' they could find. 'Perhaps I can build something to live in...'

Overnight, tramps, drug addicts and prostitutes became part of Des's family. At least they were prepared to listen to his troubles... Pretty soon, other homeless people taught him to look for food on the rubbish dump, and he found compassion in the most unlikely of places.

Des collected some pieces of cardboard scrap together to build himself a box where he could sleep, and very soon he was quite at home in his new family unit of fellow 'down and outers', including men who were prepared to steal or kill for their next fix and women who hated themselves for selling their bodies.

Living on the dump, it was not often that Des could go to school, because the teachers would start asking him questions, and he didn't want anybody to know what had happened. He felt like he couldn't do the normal things a boy of his age would do, but at least he began to feel like he belonged somewhere at last.

Yet something cried out deep within him, 'God, where are You? There must be something better for my life than this. Surely this is not my destiny?'

For three months the young boy cried out to the Lord, day and night: 'God, I don't know who You are, I don't know where Your house is, I don't know how to find You, but if You are God, You should be able to hear me. If You created the world, You must be around somewhere. Please talk to me!'

Des desperately wanted the Lord to reveal Himself or at least send somebody to give him the answers he was seeking, and yet his prayers seemed to be falling on deaf ears. And as much as he wanted to speak to somebody, anything to do with the Church was out of the question.

His father had instilled in him a dislike of Christians, often telling Des that they were a bunch of hypocrites. 'Don't go near those guys – they're bad news!' his father had constantly maintained.

So, Des turned to the prostitutes and drug-lords who were looking out for him, and began to ask them if there was such a thing as a God. 'Yes, we believe there is a God,' was the answer from everyone he spoke to, 'but we don't where He is or how to find Him. We would like to find Him too, but we don't know how.'

'Well, I'm looking for Him,' said Des, sharing his innermost desire, and even as he scrounged the dump for something to eat, he continued to pray and ask God to speak to him. Then one night as he was sitting in his box-like, make-shift home, a wind began to blow around his head. He was sitting in the dark, and yet, all of a sudden a light appeared.

'What's this?' thought Des. His first reaction was to run away, but he was not afraid – in fact, he felt a sense of peace come over him. Then he heard a voice speaking to him, a voice he has come to know over the years as the voice of God:

'My son, I know you by name. Before you were even formed in your mother's womb, I knew you. Before you were born, I set you apart and I appointed you for such a time as this, to speak on My behalf and tell other people about Me...

'I will raise you up and you will be a prophet and evangelist to the nations of the world. You will go from place to place, you will sit at the feet of kings and you will proclaim My glory to them.'

'But Lord, who am I?' replied Des. 'I am only a child and I don't know what to say. I don't know You, I don't know anything about You. I believe – but how will all this happen?

'Just obey Me. Obey My commands and I will be with you. And it will be the great I AM who will bring these things about in your life. I will place My words within your mouth and I will be with you. Now go!'

'Where am I to go, what am I to do?' Des thought to himself, trying to come to terms with this extraordinary experience. Then he remembered that his grandmother had a Bible and she had told him that it was 'God's Word to man'. Deep down in his heart it instantly dawned on him that he had to find a Bible, and so he went searching the dump for anything that looked vaguely like a book.

'God, I need your Word,' he prayed. 'There has got to be a Bible on this dump somewhere.' But after four hours of scrounging through all kinds of rubbish, he had found nothing – there were many books, but no Bible. Then, as he looked up, he saw a man dumping a whole lot of 'new' stuff. Des ran over to have a look and rummaged through many different articles until he came to a small, rectangular, brown box, which looked like it could contain a book.

'Open the box,' came that same voice again. 'My Word is in it!'

Des opened the box and inside it was a brand-new NIV Study Bible, still wrapped in its cellophane. He was overjoyed and began to thank God for this miracle – nothing like this had ever happened in his life. God was so clearly watching over him from heaven. And there have been many other miracles in his life since then.

The only problem was, he couldn't read very well. 'God, You have given me this Bible, but what does it say?' Des asked the Lord. 'This is far above my reading level – I can't understand this!' he cried, closing the book in frustration. 'What good is this to me?'

But as he pondered, Des remembered the promise the Lord had given him, that He would place His words in his mouth. 'Tell me what this says, God,' he asked as he took up the Bible, again ... the pages falling open to Jeremiah 1:4–5 by no coincidence:

> *Then the Word of the Lord came to me, saying:*
> *'Before I formed you in the womb I knew you;*
> *Before you were born I sanctified you; I ordained*
> *you a prophet to the nations.'*

Des didn't have a clue who Jeremiah was, but slowly he was able to make out some of the words, as they became illuminated in front of his eyes. 'It says You knew Jeremiah before he was born – that's what you told me,' Des said to the Lord. 'It says You appointed him to be a prophet to the nations. Lord, that's what you said to me!'

'That's right,' answered God. 'That is what I told you, and it is written in My Word.'

'Wow! Thank you, God!' Des prayed as faith began to rise up within him. And from that day forward, every time he turned to a page in the Bible, different verses would light up, as if they had been highlighted with a marker pen.

Des would struggle as best he could to understand what the Scriptures contained, but then the meaning would somehow come into his mind, and his reading rapidly improved by spending time in God's Word constantly.

Still, it was all very confusing for the young boy. 'Who is Your Son, Lord?' Des asked one day after reading John 3:16. 'It's great that You love me and that You sent Your

Son, but who is He? And how could You sacrifice Him? How could You do that? I mean, my father is a hard man, but he didn't kill me – at least he gave me a chance to run. Yet You killed Your own Son!'

In his childlike understanding, it seemed that God was a very hard taskmaster.

'You don't understand,' the Lord shared with Des, correcting his childish notions. 'I sent My Son so that you can be right with Me. His blood takes away the sins of many, and because of My Son's blood you can walk with Me and hear Me. And that is how I am able to place My words within you, because of My Son's blood which was shed for your sin.'

Des was overwhelmed by these experiences with God, and ran around telling all the prostitutes and drug addicts what had happened: 'Hey, man, I saw this light…'

'What stuff are you on, mate?' the addicts asked him. 'Sounds like it's good hash, man. Where did you get it from?'

'Hey, I'm no druggie and I don't want any of that stuff. This is real – this is God!'

'Yeah, right! We'll find out where you're getting it from!'

Despite the fact that they did not believe him, Des was extremely excited, and kept reading more of the Bible each day. 'Lord, tell me more!' was his daily plea.

'I have told you this so that you will go and tell others,' the Lord said to him. 'Why should I tell you anything more unless you are prepared to go and do what I have told you? Now go and tell others who have not heard, and if you do, I will reveal more things to you.'

And so witnessing for God became a foundation of Des Sinclair's life. He took his Bible and went off to tell everyone that they were sinners and they needed to repent if they were to escape hell's clutches and go to heaven.

'God says you are already condemned,' he said to one of the drug-lords, striking up a conversation. 'God's hand is against you because you have rejected his Son, and you will burn in hell. You need Jesus!'

Needless to say, this hardened criminal did not take too kindly to this young upstart preaching at him. After all, he was one of the top gang leaders in the area.

'But Jesus did not come to condemn you,' Des continued. 'He has come to set you free!'

The drug-crazed gangster pulled out a gun.

'Well, young man,' he said, holding the revolver to Des's head, 'I hope you know your God, because you are going to see Him in a few minutes, if He exists.'

Without further discussion or any hint of remorse, the drug-pusher pulled the trigger.

But the bullet never fired.

Once, again, he pulled the trigger, but again nothing happened.

'Stay there – don't move – don't run!' the drug-lord commanded, opening up the gun chamber to see what was going on. The pistol was fully loaded – nothing appeared to be wrong.

'Now I am going to pull it again,' he said. 'It's going to work this time!' But the gun refused to co-operate.

Trembling with fear, Des knew he had to try to escape, and before he knew it, he had taken his Bible and bashed the man over the head with it. Then he made a run for it as his opponent crumbled to the ground.

Des was literally running for his life, when the voice came to him again: *'Where are you going?'*

'I'm running for my life – I'm a dead man! Look what

You have done! You told me to go and tell people about Jesus, and now this man's after me and he's going to kill me. I'm out of here!'

'*Stop, and look behind you!*' said the voice of the Lord.

Many different thoughts were racing in Des's mind as he ran, but as he turned his head to look around, he saw that the drug-lord was strewn out on the ground. Des took this as an opportunity to continue running and secure his escape.

But the Lord had more to say: '*Stop and go back where you belong*. Go back to him.'

'But God, if I go back to him, and if he comes round, I'm a dead man!'

'Go back to him, and speak to him. My Spirit is upon him and I am with you. Now go!'

Des returned to the man, who by now was crying on the ground like a baby.

'I'm sorry I hit you,' Des said, "cause Jesus loves you.'

'You didn't hit me,' the drug-lord replied in between sobs. 'There was a man beside you who touched me, and some kind of power threw me to the ground. I *am* a sinner! I *am* wicked! Thank you for telling me this good news about Jesus.'

And so the two of them got on their knees and began to pray together. Des shared a simple prayer with him, asking God to forgive the man for his sins. He then got up after the prayer and started yelling, 'I'm free! I'm free!'

A short while later he confided in Des: 'I've got to stop dealing drugs, and go and tell all the people that I supply,' he said. 'I have to tell everyone that I have met Jesus and ask them for forgiveness. They need Jesus as well. Come with me – let's go!'

And so transformation began to break out across the rubbish dump and its wider community as Des ministered along with his first convert, praying for everyone who was willing. And the same thing that had happened to the former drug-pusher began to happen to everyone Des prayed for.

People began to fall under the power of God as Des did what seemed right to him at the time, by first praying and then bashing each one over the head with his Bible! This was all Des knew, and it had worked for the drug-lord! Although Des's methods were somewhat primitive, God still used his childlike faith, and many were set free from drug addiction.

As increasing numbers of people started gathering, hungry to know more about God, so a church was formed with an eleven-year-old boy as its pastor! 'You must bring a message to us! You must tell us what God is saying to us. We must learn,' became the cry of Des's instant congregation.

'All I can tell you is what I think God is saying to me,' Des shared, as he began to preach more and more, telling his new converts all that the Lord was showing him on a daily basis.

Back home his mother was longing for him, and did try to make contact with him a number of times, but Des would avoid her because he knew it would only cause her further pain, if his father found out.

Looking back at his childhood today, Des has forgiven his earthly father, and his relationship with his parents has been completely restored. In hindsight, he is grateful to his heavenly Father for his extraordinary childhood, which has positioned him for ministry today in such a unique way, teaching him to rely totally on God from a very young age and to expect the Lord to show up in signs and wonders.

'God has got a funny way of getting us where He wants us to be, and it is never the way we think or expect,' says

Des. 'But this was the way the Lord had to get me to a place where I could meet Him, and I am so grateful for that.'

Where are you in your walk with God right now? If you do not yet know the Lord Jesus Christ as Lord and Saviour, take a few moments to pray the following prayer of salvation and like the drug-lord in this story your life can also be miraculously changed.

A prayer of salvation

> *Lord Jesus, I believe that You are the Son of God,*
> *that You went to the cross and shed Your blood*
> *for my sin.*
> *Lord, I recognize that I am a sinner and repent of*
> *my sins.*
> *I claim Your precious blood and receive complete*
> *forgiveness.*
> *I give You authority over my spirit, my soul and*
> *my body.*
> *And I ask You to be Lord of my life and to teach*
> *me and guide me so that I can follow Your ways.*
> *Holy Spirit, I ask You to come and reveal all truth*
> *to me and help me to follow Jesus.*
> *In the name of Jesus, Amen.*

Or perhaps you have served the Lord for many years, but have become tired and weary in your faith. If that is how you are feeling today, take heart. God has a plan and a purpose especially for your life – a divine destiny that He wants to launch you into. What he has accomplished in the life of Des Sinclair, He can also do for you.

God Almighty can reach down from heaven into your desperation and despair and give you hope. He says:

*For I know the thoughts that I think toward you,
says the Lord, thoughts of peace and not of evil, to
give you a future and a hope. Then you will call
upon Me and go and pray to Me, and I will listen
to you.*

Jeremiah 29:11–12

In God, the homeless can find shelter and believers can defy death. As you continue to read, may faith rise up in your heart. Now is the time to trust the Lord for the impossible!

Chapter 3

The God Who Answers
with Fire

GHANA

'If the Lord is God, follow Him; but if Baal, follow him.'

1 Kings 18:21

'Either your Jesus is God, and He will bring our brother back to life, or He is a liar and you will all die! If your God proves to us that He is real by raising the dead, our whole tribe will bow down and worship Him. But if not, we will kill you all.'

The words of the Muslim tribal leader cut deep into Des Sinclair like a knife. Des was not sure if he was up for a challenge like this, especially with such high stakes. How would the Lord come through for him this time?

A corpse lay in front of him and Des knew he had to act quickly, otherwise he and his colleagues would be sharing the same fate. This was West Africa and these men were not joking...

But how could he put God to the test like this? And yet, what an opportunity for the Lord to act and bring salvation to so many...

Eight months before, the Lord had miraculously delivered Des from that Muslim jail in Mali, and now, as he continued to preach in the marketplaces and churches of Ghana, it was as if this was a direct retaliation of the devil, now that he was back in West Africa.

And once again, the everyday ministry of the young evangelist was to have extraordinary biblical parallels – this time from the Old Testament, as 1 Kings 18:21–40 literally began to unfold before Des:

The God who answers by fire

And Elijah came to all the people, and said, 'How long will you falter between two opinions? If the Lord is God, follow Him; but if Baal, follow him.' But the people answered him not a word. Then Elijah said to the people, 'I alone am left a prophet of the Lord; but Baal's prophets are four hundred and fifty men. Therefore let them give us two bulls; and let them choose one bull for themselves, cut it in pieces, and lay it on the wood, but put no fire under it; and I will prepare the other bull, and lay it on the wood, but put no fire under it. Then you call on the name of your gods, and I will call on the name of the Lord; and the God who answers by fire, He is God.'

So all the people answered and said, 'It is well spoken.' Now Elijah said to the prophets of Baal, 'Choose one bull for yourselves and prepare it first, for you are many; and call on the name of your god, but put no fire under it.' So they took the bull which was given them, and they prepared it, and called on the name of Baal from morning even till noon, saying, 'O Baal, hear us!' But there was no voice; no one answered. Then they leaped about the altar which they had made.

And so it was, at noon, that Elijah mocked them and said, 'Cry aloud, for he is a god; either he is meditating, or he is busy, or he is on a journey, or perhaps he is sleeping and must be awakened.' So they cried aloud, and cut themselves, as was their custom, with knives and lances, until the blood gushed out on them. And when midday was past, they prophesied until the time of the offering of the evening sacrifice. But there was no voice; no one answered, no one paid attention.

Then Elijah said to all the people, 'Come near to me.' So all the people came near to him. And he repaired the altar of the Lord that was broken down. And Elijah took twelve stones... [and] built an altar in the name of the Lord; and he made a trench around the altar large enough to hold two seahs of seed. And he put the wood in order, cut the bull in pieces, and laid it on the wood, and said, 'Fill four waterpots with water, and pour it on the burnt sacrifice and on the wood.' Then he said, 'Do it a second time,' and they did it a second time; and he said, 'Do it a third time,' and they did it a third time. So the water ran all around the altar; and he also filled the trench with water.

And it came to pass, at the time of the offering of the evening sacrifice, that Elijah the prophet came near and said, 'Lord God of Abraham, Isaac, and Israel, let it be known this day that You are God in Israel and I am Your servant, and that I have done all these things at Your word. Hear me,

*O Lord, hear me, that this people may know that
You are the Lord God, and that You have turned
their hearts back to You again.'*

*Then the fire of the Lord fell and consumed
the burnt sacrifice, and the wood and the stones
and the dust, and it licked up the water that was
in the trench. Now when all the people saw it, they
fell on their faces; and they said, 'The Lord, He
is God! The Lord, He is God!' And Elijah said to
them, 'Seize the prophets of Baal! Do not let one
of them escape!' So they seized them; and Elijah
brought them down to the Brook Kishon and
executed them there.*

During his first trip to West Africa, Des was in Ghana for
eight weeks, and following his miraculous escape from
Mali, was preaching in and around churches in Accra and
Kumasi as well as in the bustling marketplaces.

It was nothing unusual for him to preach six times
on a Sunday, one service after another. One particular
Sunday, he had already preached twice, when he was
taken to the Lighthouse Revival Centre, a large church
building in Kumasi, where he felt the Lord had given him
a specific message.

Des always trusts the Lord for a word in season for
each congregation he ministers to, and for this particular
church, he felt God wanted to show them His glory. As
Des started his message, the Lord started to speak to him:
'This is My word to this church, and I will show you My
glory through it. Now preach on Lazarus being raised
from the dead...'

'But Lord, it is the people who need to see a
manifestation of Your glory, not me,' Des thought. Anyway,

he began to share how unbelievers are dead in Christ
before they are born again, but that, just as Jesus called
Lazarus forth, so the Lord calls each person to salvation
in Him through His shed blood. And as they received the
Lord Jesus, they would no longer be dead, but would have
new life in Christ.

Little did Des realize that a dead man was being
brought to him at that very time, and in a few moments his
message would be totally interrupted. 'If I had known this,'
he later confided, 'I wouldn't have preached about Lazarus
coming forth from the dead – I wouldn't have even gone
near it!'

Des opened his Bible to John 11 and started reading:

Now a certain man was sick, Lazarus of Bethany,
the town of Mary and her sister Martha...

As he got to verse 40, he began to hear a noise outside, but
he just kept reading all the louder:

Jesus said to her, 'Did I not say to you that if you
would believe you would see the glory of God?'
Then they took away the stone from the place
where the dead man was lying. And Jesus lifted up
His eyes and said, 'Father, I thank You that You
have heard Me. And I know that You always hear
Me, but because of the people who are standing
by I said this, that they may believe that You sent
Me.'

'Verse 43,' Des continued, trying to be heard above the
commotion going on outside the building:

*Now when He had said these things, He cried with
a loud voice, 'Lazarus, come forth!' And he who
had died came out bound hand and foot with grave
clothes, and his face was wrapped with a cloth.
Jesus said to them, 'Loose him, and let him go.'*

Then all of a sudden, the back doors of the church opened
and a crowd of men dressed in Muslim religious clothing
barged in. They were carrying somebody on a stretcher.

Des looked to Pastor Emmanuel, the leader of the
church, for some explanation of what was going on,
especially since he saw the men were carrying weapons
and had blocked the door behind them. The pastor quickly
addressed the men in the local language:

'Why are you here? What do you want?' he asked.

'We are here because of *that man*,' said one of the
Muslims, pointing to Des. And so an extraordinary story
began to unfold.

While Des had been spending a lot of time preaching
in the marketplace in Kumasi, sharing the Gospel and
praying for the sick, he was totally unaware that a radical
Islamist was listening to his every word and was plotting
against him.

Committed to waging *jihad* against Christians, the
so-called 'infidels', he had even drawn a sketch of Des to
identify him to other radical Muslims, so they could take
action against him.

But the Lord clearly wanted to reach down to this dear
man in all his bitterness and heal his physical deformity. He
had been born a hunchback, and was bent over with one
leg shorter than the other and a huge lump on his back.

While Des had been praying for the sick, days before,
he had asked people to put their hands on the parts of

the body where they were unwell. 'The Spirit of God is moving among the crowd now. God is healing people!' he had shouted excitedly. Then, he had had a profound word of knowledge.

'There is a man here. You are a hunchback and God wants to heal you. You are a Muslim, and I break that spirit of deception over your life right now. God has a plan and a purpose for you and is releasing you from your disability, right now. Be straightened in the name of Jesus!'

The moment Des had said that, the man's back had automatically come into proper alignment, his legs had grown and he had stood up completely whole, all within a few seconds. Tears had started to roll down his face and he had felt the warm presence of the love of God touching him.

'I was instantly healed,' the man later shared with Des, telling him the whole story, but at the time he was so shocked, he literally bolted out of the marketplace to return home to his family in the northern part of the country. They were just as astonished when they saw him come into the house.

However, the jubilation of his miraculous transformation was short lived. As fate would have it, the man's brother had just died of cerebral malaria and the family were in mourning and making plans for an immediate burial, in line with their religious tradition.

'You went away from us a hunchback, but you've come back a whole man,' his father said to him. 'How can this be?'

'All I can tell you is that this white man prayed for me, and this Jesus came and touched me, and I felt a wind come upon me. Now look at me! We know that these Christians claim that their Jesus can raise people from the dead. Perhaps he can also raise my brother from the dead, just as he has healed me.'

And so a major debate ensued among the family and community leaders. Finally they agreed to break with custom and not bury the dead man immediately, but to take him to Kumasi to find Des, so he could be prayed for.

However, the tribal chief had given the condition that if the dead man was not brought back to life, then Des would have to be killed as a false prophet, but if the man was raised from the dead, then the whole community would renounce Islam and follow Jesus.

'Either Your Jesus will bring our brother back to life,' the Muslim tribal leader had repeated, 'or He is a liar and you will all die!'

The men had then travelled for several days with the dead body, before they finally reached Kumasi and the church where Des was preaching. Now, once again, the young evangelist was faced with an opportunity to be overwhelmed with fear.

'Lord, get me out of here!' he prayed under his breath. 'I am going to have to make a run for it,' he thought to himself, thinking about the rear exit behind the pulpit. 'I don't have this kind of faith. I have never seen a dead man raised back to life. I know it's in the Bible, but I don't know if I believe I can raise a dead man. It's not my gifting or my calling...

'Lord, this isn't fair! Why have You allowed this to happen? Especially since I have just read the Scripture about Lazarus to the people – now I'm faced with the real thing! Lord, help me to persuade them to give us more time to get hold of the world-renowned evangelist, Reinhard Bonnke, or someone with the gift of working miracles to raise this dead man. Lord, if you don't raise him up, we are all dead, and Your name will be mocked.'

Deep in his heart Des knew that God was well able to raise the dead, but in his head, he wasn't so sure. What a dilemma to be faced with.

Pastor Emmanuel motioned for the men to bring the dead man forward. He was now eight and a half days dead and they placed the stretcher right in front of the pulpit where Des was preaching. In the hot African climate, the stench was unbearable.

'Let's continue,' he instructed the congregation.

'Lord, the smell is so bad, I want to vomit!' Des whispered to the Lord as he tried to remember the next point of his message, his knees knocking beneath him. 'Lord, You have got to do something!'

Des began to pray over the corpse, casting away the spirit of death, praying fervently in the name of Jesus – but nothing happened.

He continued to share about the promises of the Word of God and how they can be received by faith, at this stage feeling like a complete hypocrite. Then once again he began to pray for the dead man, shaking him vigorously and breathing life into him seven times. He called him forth and rebuked the devil, doing everything he could humanly think of… but still nothing happened.

The third time, Des invited the pastor to pray with him. At this stage he was desperate. Then Pastor Emmanuel looked at him and said something profound:

'Get your eyes off the dead man,' he instructed, 'and get your eyes on the living Jesus Christ. Preach the Word of Life, and I tell you the truth – you shall shake this man's hand before you leave here today.'

Des began to pray and asked the Lord to forgive him. 'I'm sorry, Lord, for doubting you, and trying to do things in my own strength.' And as he turned his eyes back on

Jesus, the Spirit of God began to manifest in the service and miracles started to break out across the room.

Blind eyes started to see, deaf ears started to hear, disabled people starting running around the building, and great excitement broke forth across the congregation as people began to get healed in their seats.

Des was mightily encouraged. 'Thank you, Lord. You're back with me!'

'I never left you,' the Lord said. 'You left Me.'

After a half hour of praying for the sick, and the Lord moving so powerfully, Des now felt confident to pray for the dead man once again, but he could not be found. The stretcher was no longer in front of the pulpit.

'Where is the dead man?' he asked the pastor. 'Bring him back – I want to pray for him. I have the faith now.'

'He's not dead any more!' Pastor Emmanuel replied.

'Where is he?' Des asked, not comprehending what the pastor was saying. 'I want to try again!'

'He's alive!' the pastor said, trying to explain.

'I want to pray for him!'

'You mean you would you like to meet him?' asked Emmanuel.

Then a man came walking towards Des from the back of the church. The glory of God was radiating all over his body. His face was shining and his eyes were like piercing laser beams.

Des could hardly recognize him. When he had prayed for this man, he had been a mass of rotting flesh. Now his skin was perfect and shining.

As Des took the man's hand, it was like an electric shock went through his body, and he was thrown backwards into the air. When he tried to get up, he could hardly move, the presence of the Lord was so strong.

Now the Lord reminded Des of the promise the men had made, that if Jesus was proved to be God, they would bow down and serve Him. 'Lord, give me the strength to stand up and call these men forward and hold them to their word,' he prayed.

Des managed to get up and address the men, leading them in the sinner's prayer. One by one, they dropped their weapons and got on their knees to recognize Jesus Christ as God, and renounce Allah. Each of them repented of their sins and gave their lives to the Lord, with the full understanding that they now faced the death sentence from radical Islam, for turning away from the Muslim faith and following Jesus Christ.

But the Lord wasn't finished with them. He knew the heavy price these converts had to pay, and He began to give Des a word of encouragement to prophesy over the men:

'God has raised this man up from the dead to show you that *He* is not dead – He is alive! And now, as this man's shadow falls upon men, they will see Jesus and be healed.

'What was once the hunter, will now become the hunted. You will know what it is like to suffer for Christ's name, but God will be with you!'

And so a whole community in West Africa was impacted by the Gospel literally overnight, as God answered by resurrection fire.

Today Des and Ros still carry a great burden for people of other faiths in their hearts, knowing that it is only through the signs and wonders that follow the preaching of the Word of God that the devotees of other religions will be swayed from their radical position.

Chapter 4

A Bright Light in the Darkness

South Africa

You shall be called the Repairer of the Breach.

If you extend your soul to the hungry
And satisfy the afflicted soul,
Then your light shall dawn in the darkness,
And your darkness shall be as the noonday.
The Lord will guide you continually,
And satisfy your soul in drought,
And strengthen your bones;
You shall be like a watered garden,
And like a spring of water, whose waters do not
fail.
Those from among you
Shall build the old waste places;
You shall raise up the foundations of many
generations;
And you shall be called the Repairer of the
Breach,
The Restorer of Streets to Dwell In.

Isaiah 58:10–12

Des Sinclair was eleven-years-old when he started preaching the Gospel, and eighteen when he was ordained as a minister to an independent church in Australia, clearly illustrating how the Lord can dynamically raise up the youth of today to reach the lost, the lonely and the hurting, and transform the communities they live in.

Des's encounter with God on that rubbish dump in New Zealand is something that has impacted his life ever since. It was there that he learnt to hear the Lord's voice, and where the Lord ignited a passion within him to reach people of all walks of life, and especially those who other preachers could not be bothered with.

Just as Jesus had taken the loaves and fishes of a young boy, and multiplied what he had in his hand to feed the multitudes, it was as if the Lord had taken what little a homeless boy had in his heart, to spiritually nourish a congregation of 1,500 people, who gathered each Sunday on the dump to receive the bread of life.

It was through this homeless crowd of street-dwellers, prostitutes and drug addicts, that the Lord would lead Des to understand the extent of His love and compassion for fallen people, and a Scripture would begin to burn on his heart, which today encapsulates all that he and Ros stand for, through their ministry, which has come to be known as Life Evangelism International. The Scripture was Isaiah 58:10–12:

> *If you extend your soul to the hungry and satisfy the afflicted soul, then your light shall dawn in the darkness, and your darkness shall be as the noonday... you shall build the old waste places; and you shall be called the Repairer of the Breach, the Restorer of Streets to Dwell In.*

It is this Scripture which has inspired Des to visit more than thirty nations thus far, including West Africa, where God delivered him so mightily out of the clutches of radical Islam in Mali and Ghana, and where he saw God's resurrection power in action to transform a whole community.

And it is this Scripture which still inspires Des and Ros today, as 'Repairers of the Breach', ministers of reconciliation who are devoted to bringing people back into relationship with the Lord, and 'Restorers of Streets to Dwell In' who are committed to rebuilding a just and humane society.

God had taken a homeless young boy under His wing and begun to teach him the ways of the Lord, in the most unlikely of places – a rubbish dump on the wrong side of town. But the Lord knew Des could not fulfil his divine calling alone. He needed a father in the faith, and the loving arms of a family to provide for him and support him in his spiritual growth.

Yes, revival was breaking out on the rubbish dump in Des's home town, but the Lord had not just called him to Levin, or New Zealand, but to the nations, and it was time for him to take his next step in God. It was at this time that the Brown family came into his life.

Des and Ros first met when her father, Gordon Brown, a pastor in a Pentecostal church in Levin, took the boy preacher into his home, where he lived for a short period of time.

Impressed by Des's potential for ministry, Pastor Gordon felt led to take the twelve-year-old boy under his wing, not only helping him to complete his education, but also providing the budding young evangelist with a wonderful godly role model.

During this time Des was sent back to school, and he and Ros became friends through their mutual love of music. Little did they realize then that they would one day be ministering around the world together, for love and marriage would only come much later – in fact, after Des had returned from a number of years ministering in Australia, following one of the most tragic periods of his life.

A fearless young woman, Ros Brown grew up in the New Zealand countryside near the town of Foxton, where her parents had a dairy farm before they moved into full-time ministry. Growing up in a Christian family, she always had a close relationship with the Lord Jesus, and as a farmer's daughter, she loved helping her dad in the fields.

Though New Zealand was a comparatively safe country to be raised in, it seems that the enemy already recognized Ros's future potential, as he tried to wipe her out a number of times.

As a young girl she was nearly killed in a tractor accident one winter morning, as she helped her dad collect hay to feed the cattle. One minute the tractor was motoring slowly forward, and the next it was on its side with two wheels spinning in the air, and Ros was thrown into a large ditch.

Gordon was distraught as he looked for his daughter, but she was nowhere to be found, and tears started to roll down his cheeks. Fortunately Ros was not injured and soon came scrambling out of the ditch. Her clothes were full of mud, but she had miraculously survived.

'I saw my dad standing at the top of the ditch and he was crying his eyes out,' Ros recalls. 'The whole incident upset him greatly and it was a long time before he let me back on the tractor again!'

Later, as a teenager, Ros was nearly run over by an oncoming truck as she rode her bicycle to work at a sewing factory where she was a machinist.

'I was coming down a very steep hill,' she recalls, 'and

almost lost control of my bike as it sped towards the middle of the road and the oncoming traffic. A large truck was heading straight for me and it should have run me over, but somehow I was able to steer myself back to safety. I truly believe the Lord was my protector in this incident and that He sent angels to save my life.'

Indeed, Ros had learnt to trust in the protection of God at a young age, and to be in tune with His guidance and to heed His warnings. One such warning came in the form of a prophetic dream her father experienced over a number of nights.

Ros' parents were with The Salvation Army at the time, and had a heart for Africa. In fact, they were planning to sell their farm and go to Zimbabwe as missionaries, as they felt they could make a difference teaching the local people farming.

At the time the country was known as Rhodesia and was embroiled in a bloody war, where many innocent civilians were losing their lives on a daily basis. Despite this, the Browns were about to join a Christian mission station in the Bulawayo region. But just before they were about to depart, Gordon had a recurring dream warning them not to go.

He dreamt that he and his family had not long arrived at the mission station, when rebel soldiers surrounded the mission and opened fire on the missionaries stationed there as well as the workers on the farm, and tragically they were all slaughtered.

This same dream troubled Gordon for a number of nights, and he eventually went to speak to some of the leaders in The Salvation Army, who advised him to postpone going to Africa for the time being. The family were understandably disappointed – especially Ros, as she believed God had called her family to impact Africa in some way... But then they received the awful news.

The mission station they were heading for had been attacked by terrorists and there were no survivors – exactly as her father had dreamt would happen.

'If we had gone, my family would have been there exactly one week before the attack,' Ros recalls today, 'and there is no doubt we would all have been killed. Every man, woman and child on that mission station was murdered.

'So, if my dad had not been in tune with what God was saying to us, we would all be dead today. So, yes, Satan has tried to take out my family and kill me, just like he has tried to do many times with Des.

'But the devil did not win then, and neither will he prevail against us in the future. Not only were my family and I saved from certain disaster, but our dream to reach Africa has now been realized through Life Evangelism International.

'My parents may never have come to Africa or ministered in Zimbabwe, but I have travelled throughout the continent, and Des and I have ministered in Zimbabwe many times.

'I have always had a soft spot in my heart for this African nation, ever since that time, and the Lord used the whole incident as a seed, way back then, to fulfil that calling on my family, today.'

So, right from a young age, Ros had a passion and calling for Africa and to be a part of the miraculous. Like David the shepherd boy, who killed a lion and a bear long before he tackled Goliath, it was experiences like these that prepared her for ministry in Africa and some of the situations that she and her husband would later encounter, which could have easily left her paralysed by fear.

But Ros learnt to overcome her fears as a young woman: 'Early on in my life, I came to the realization that there is nothing to be afraid of when you are serving Jesus. And through experiences like these, I knew God was with me and had looked after me, and so there was no need for me to be scared.

'If one has a simple child-like faith, which is what I believe I have, then you have no problem believing God's promises to us in the Scriptures. If God says it, I believe it, and that's all there is to it. The Lord has spoken and that is good enough for me.

'I know God is with me and His angels are protecting me, and so, as Des and I go into Africa, whatever circumstances we face, we are not afraid. Yes, we go through some horrendous situations and there are times when I am a bit nervous, but I'm not fearful, because God is with me.'

Des and Ros always seek the Lord before they go anywhere, believing that just as Ros's father had been warned not to go to Zimbabwe, God will show them clearly if it is not the right time to visit a particular nation.

'There are times when I can accompany Des into certain countries,' Ros says, 'and other times when I feel prompted in my Spirit to remain behind. We have to be constantly led by the Holy Spirit in all that we do.'

Des was twelve-years-old when he came to live with the Browns and Ros was sixteen, and although there was a four-year age gap, they soon became good friends. 'When Des came into our church, he started to learn how to play the drums,' says Ros, 'so we had a lot to talk about, through our common interest in music, and we found it very easy to communicate with each other.

'We were just friends then, but a number of years later,

when Des returned from Australia, our friendship began to blossom as we realized we had more in common than just music, including our shared vision for Africa.'

When Pastor Peter Whitcombe married Des and Ros Sinclair in New Zealand on 16 February 1991, little did he realize that it wasn't just a young couple joining their lives together, but the birth of a ministry that would impact the nations.

They both had learnt to overcome their doubts and fears and trust God completely to lead them, whatever the situation – whether stepping out in faith to share the Gospel in a scary situation, or overcoming their initial reticence to pray for a sick person, or moving to another country.

For this young couple, life was about living, and they were not going to be held back by negative reports of all that could go wrong. They were simply going to step out in faith and live life to the full, trusting God for his abundant life and provision to flow through their lives.

Their early ministry together was a time when the Lord used them to help plant a number of churches and to work with young people. But all the while, the call to Africa was becoming increasingly clear.

God had called Des on the rubbish dump to be a prophet to the nations, and when he was water-baptized at the age of twelve in the Pentecostal Church in Levin, he received a detailed call to Africa. An apostolic prophet from New Zealand prophesied over him that he would go to a dark continent, far away across the ocean, which was scorched by the sun and where there was very little water.

'You will go to the southern tip of Africa,' he prophesied, 'a land which is full of controversy, which the whole world has rejected because of its government's policies.

'God will send you there, and you will be based in that

land, and He will use you to go from city to city, town to town and place to place, to bring revival. And you will take with you men who you are discipling, and you will release them into the work of the ministry.

'You will be like nomads, but you will preach the Gospel to a sea of humanity, and from South Africa you will travel into Africa and other nations all over the world.

'You will also address leaders in high places – those in government, prime ministers, tribal leaders and kings, and hundreds of thousands of people will come into My Kingdom because of your obedience and faithfulness.'

Later, God would send a Ghanaian believer by the name of Yaw to live in Ros and Des's home, while he ministered in New Zealand for a season and attended Bible school in Tauranga. It was this young African minister who would constantly rekindle their interest in the continent of Africa, as he shared about his homeland and invited them to come and minister in Ghana.

Then in June 1997, Des went to Africa for the first time to attend the Global Consultation on World Evangelization conference (GCOWE) in Pretoria. As more than a thousand ministers from all across Africa were gathered there, he realized this was an excellent opportunity, and he could also use it to take advantage of Yaw's invitation to minister in Ghana.

It was during this trip that Des met up with a number of ministers from West Africa, who invited him to Burkina Faso, Benin, Senegal, Togo, Ivory Coast and Nigeria. It was also during this first African trip that Des was invited by an international ministry organization to relocate to South Africa and help to train up young evangelists, an invitation that would be extended three times over the next six months.

Finally, in 1998, the Lord sent prophets from Kansas City to confirm Des and Ros's call to Africa. These Americans almost repeated the prophecy Des had received as a boy, word for word. The prophets were speaking at a conference in Tauranga, and when Des did not attend, as he was seeking the Lord for direction, they came knocking on his door.

'There is an evangelist in this town, who is not here,' one of the prophets had shared with the pastors of the church, describing Des in detail, 'and he has a big decision to make, and we have some direction for him.' The pastors immediately recognized who he was talking about, and took the prophets over to Des and Ros's home.

'It was prophesied over you at the age of twelve that God would send you to Africa to train up evangelists and bring revival wherever you go,' one of the prophets began. 'You would be like a nomad, travelling from place to place to preach the Gospel to a sea of people, and many would come into the Kingdom because of your call,' continued another prophet.

'God has been speaking to you and you have made the right decision, not to go to Zimbabwe and pick up the call there, but to go to South Africa and be based there. God is trying to get your attention, because three times you have been approached to come. Now is the time to "turn the page" and go!'

This was a remarkable confirmation, as the Sinclairs were already planning to pack up and head for South Africa. 'We hadn't mentioned our plans to anyone else at the time,' Ros remembers, 'but we felt within our hearts that a fresh season was upon us, that it was time to turn the page... and these were the very words the prophets used! So that really captured our attention.'

Finally, in September 1998 the Sinclairs moved to Johannesburg, where they have been ever since, raising up young pastors and evangelists, and being involved in humanitarian work, HIV/AIDS awareness as part of evangelistic training, mass outdoor Gospel crusades, Catch the Fire conferences and healing crusades across Southern Africa. From South Africa they continue to make inroads into the continent of Africa and the nations of the world.

They truly believe that God has called them to repair the breach, build up the waste places and raise up outcasts, and in their passionate quest to help others to find breakthroughs, they have many documented reports of how God has healed people through their ministry all over Africa. Many of these amazing healing testimonies can be read at the Life Evangelism International website, www.lei.org.za, complete with photographic evidence of how the Lord has used their ministry to open blind eyes and heal people who could not walk.

As an example, see the photo section showing what happened to a blind woman at Miracle Valley Church in Soshenguve township in South Africa on Easter Sunday 2002. This woman had been completely blind for four years because of a diabetes-related condition, but she came to church regularly, believing Jesus could heal her.

After Des had preached that glorious day, he had asked for all those who were sick to come forward for prayer, and this lady came walking to the front, helped by two other women. Before praying, Des did a test to see if she had any vision at all, but she did not. Then, following the example of the Lord Jesus, he took some dirt from the ground outside and made it muddy with some water.

He then took some mud and put it on the woman's eyes and prayed for her to receive her sight back in the name of Jesus. As the woman cleaned her eyes, she was completely healed. 'I can see! I can see!' she shouted with great joy.

In the photo section you can also see photos of how Des and Ros prayed for a woman at the Apostolic Faith Mission church in this same township, on another occasion, and how she got up out of her wheelchair and walked! This records just one miracle at a five-hour service on 24 March 2002, where God moved incredibly as the demonically possessed were set free, and all kinds of physical conditions were healed.

This particular lady had been unable to walk for twelve years following a car accident and was now confined to a wheelchair, as she could no longer stand or walk. Her back was broken, and several vertebrae and one of her hips were crushed. Her leg muscles had shrunk terribly and she was in constant pain. Even if she moved slightly, the agony was unbearable.

But when Des, Ros and their interpreter prayed for the woman, the Holy Spirit came upon her and the pain left completely. In fact, she started to move her legs freely. Des and Ros then left her for a few minutes to exercise her legs as they continued to pray for others, but when they went back to check up on her, she said she felt she was now able to stand up!

Des and Ros prayed for her again, and he and the interpreter helped her up out of the wheelchair, and she started to walk behind it, pushing it along for balance. Then she let her wheelchair go and started walking down the middle aisle unaided! This was a remarkable sight to see, and fortunately the pastor managed to photograph it.

Such miracles happen regularly in the ministry of Des and Ros Sinclair, because they have been obedient to the call to go and faithful to pursue it over the past ten years in Africa, and because they continue to glorify God alone for His miracle-working power.

Chapter 5

Is This What Heaven is Like?

HEAVEN (PART 1)

Death has been swallowed up in victory. Where, O death, is your sting?

1 Corinthians 15:54–55 (NIV)

While lying chained to that cold concrete floor in the prison in Mali, when it all seemed so hopeless, there was something hidden deep in Des Sinclair's heart that sustained him throughout that very dark night.

It was the same inner witness which had encouraged him not to give up in Ghana, when those armed men took control of the church he was preaching in, and demanded that he raise a dead man or die.

Many times he has literally been at death's door, at times delirious from pain and facing the temptation to just let go of his life. After all, in every one of these experiences he has known exactly where he was going – straight to heaven to be with the Father in glory – and yet he has also known, deep within, that his work on earth was not yet over.

Des's death sentence in Mali was not the first time he had experienced such a near encounter with death, nor would it be the last. He had experienced a major health attack as a seventeen-year-old boy and had been rushed to hospital, and it is a miracle that he ever came out alive.

In 1987, while Des was still living on New Zealand's North Island, he moved from Levin to take up a ministry call in Tokoroa, a heavily forested town in the hub of the country's massive timber industry. This was where Ros's father was pastoring a Pentecostal church, and Des had been invited to serve alongside his future father-in-law as he continued to train for the ministry.

And what a good training ground this would prove to be, with so much spiritual opposition facing the local Christian community, with many witch covens in the area and much sorcery being practised by indigenous witchdoctors. The only way to tackle this was through extended periods of spiritual warfare. Des, Gordon and other church leaders had been fasting and praying for days when disaster struck after one Sunday morning service.

'I am not feeling at all well,' Des told his flatmates when he got back from the service. 'I think I'm going to have to go and lie down for a while.' Little did he realize that he had been hit by a sudden illness that doctors would be unable to explain or treat.

So quick was the devil's retaliation after this period of intense warfare, that Des did not realize the connection or how serious his condition was. All he knew was that his body was now burning with fever and his head was incredibly dizzy. One minute he was shivering and the next moment he was sweating.

'Lord, what's going on? Have I got a virus or something? What must I pray against?' he asked the Lord, as he began to confess every healing Scripture he could remember. He knew the power of divine healing in his life and was full of faith. Even so, he soon fell into a deep sleep, and when he woke up he hardly knew where he was. 'Something's very wrong!' he called out to one of his flatmates. 'You've got to get me to the doctor!'

His friend immediately called Pastor Gordon, who quickly came around to the flat. 'We need to get this boy to hospital,' the pastor said, the moment he saw Des's condition, which seemed to be deteriorating.

Des soon became delirious, and when the doctor at Tokoroa's hospital examined him, he immediately called for an ambulance to take Des through to a larger hospital in the neighbouring city of Hamilton, where he could be better cared for.

'Where am I?' Des asked the nurse, as he looked around the ambulance.

'Don't you know where you are?' the man replied.

'Am I in heaven?' Des questioned, almost as if he had an inner foreknowledge of what was to come.

'Well, you may not be far from it, but you are definitely still here on earth,' the nurse tried to reassure him. 'However, you are in a very serious condition and we are taking you to the intensive care unit at Hamilton Hospital.'

At that point Des lost consciousness. His blood pressure was sky high, his heartbeat was going crazy and his body was shutting down. Worst of all, when he got to the ICU, nobody knew why this was happening to him. They had never seen anything like this before and didn't have a clue about what was going on.

Then, all of a sudden, it seemed to Des as if he was looking down on the whole scene, observing the doctors and nurses in a hive of activity. He was lying on an operating table, hooked up to all kinds of machines, and his body was jerking wildly, but at the same time he was watching the whole procedure from above.

It was obvious he was going into cardiac arrest. 'What

are you doing to me? Be careful!' Des cried out to the doctors, but nobody could hear him. They kept clamping his chest, but to no avail, and the heart monitor continued to flatline. The emergency medical team tried to revive Des again and again, but there was still no movement on the monitor.

'What should I put down as the time of death?' a doctor officiously asked.

In a flash, a beam of light encompassed Des, and a huge pair of hands pulled him up into a tunnel that was so bright, he could hardly keep his eyes open. In a split second he was taken from one place to another, yet there was no fear, just an overwhelming sense of peace and belonging.

Des was overawed by the array of colours emblazoned upon the sky as he passed through the clouds. There against this extraordinary backdrop, was a huge doorway, guarded by a colossal statue on either side. They looked like great lions, yet each had six wings. It seemed they were made out of stone, grey and serene, but they were alive, with piercing eyes all over them like rubies.

As a pathway unfolded beneath Des's feet, he looked down on a cobbled road. Yet these were no ordinary bricks – they shone with a golden brilliance, and they somehow seemed to pull him in the direction he needed to be going.

As he came nearer the doorway, it was as if the massive monuments suddenly came alive and turned their heads towards him to scrutinize him carefully. It was as though every one of their piercing eyes was focused on him, like countless laser beams.

As Des passed, these living creatures looked straight through him, piercing into the very core of his being, discerning his right to be there.

But there was no fear, as the road kept pulling Des along. Then the great doors automatically opened to let him into the most magnificent garden he had ever seen. Looking across the horizon, flowers and trees stretched for miles, and Des was quite overcome by the breathtaking beauty.

In the distance he could see a brilliant light, like the sun, that seemed to get brighter all the time, radiating life and energy throughout the entire landscape and causing everything to glow.

As Des continued walking, he came towards a large lake, where a small boat was waiting for him on the shore. 'I have to get in,' he thought to himself, 'but there are no oars or paddles, and the water is completely still.'

Nevertheless, Des stepped into the boat and made himself comfortable. Then as he looked down at the crystal-clear expanse beneath him, he could see a current forming and the boat began to rock to and fro, as it was pulled across the lake towards the other side.

Des was soon joined by a school of large fish, on either side of the boat and in front of it. They seemed to be leading him in a certain direction. They were brightly coloured, some a fiery red, some speckled with white, each of them jumping in and out of the water joyously!

In the distance, Des could see a shoreline, where many people had gathered to welcome him. He felt great excitement as the boat took him closer, somehow knowing that he was about to meet his Lord and Master.

Even before the boat came to a standstill, a very tall being began to walk towards Des, offering him His hand to help him out of the boat. 'Follow Me!' He said kindly, and Des knew instinctively that this was the Lord Jesus.

'I wonder who all these people are standing on the shore,' Des thought to himself. 'They seem so familiar, almost like I know them.'

Immediately the Lord answered, although He did not

speak a word. He did not need to – what He had to say just seemed to flood Des's mind.

'That is Elijah… and there is the Apostle Paul…'

'The prophet, Elijah? Paul, the Apostle?'

'Yes… and many other men who have inspired you. You have read about their great exploits in My name and have been encouraged by them, while you have been on earth…

'They have been cheering you on, and praying for you, that you would complete the work that I have laid out for you on earth. I have brought them here because you have much to learn from them. You will spend time with them and they will show you many things.'

As Des walked away from the boat towards a beach of fine white sand, he was fascinated by the structured maze of many different golden paths ahead of him, and he knew he would have been quite lost if the Lord had not been there to show him where to go.

'Follow Me!' he heard once again, the words echoing throughout his body as they continued walking, upwards along a path that took them ever closer to the light.

On both sides of the path, Des could see many great buildings of all different kinds, stretching for miles and miles, with people everywhere – and the amazing thing was that he was entirely in tune with their thoughts.

This was a place where you did not really need to speak like on earth – you could look at a person and know exactly what they were thinking, and they immediately knew what you were thinking. Nothing was hidden here.

Children were running and playing on beautiful grassy fields, and families were joyfully interacting with each other. Everywhere he looked, Des felt total acceptance, peace and harmony – he felt completely welcome, as if he was part of each family.

'What are these large buildings?' he asked the Lord. 'They look like houses, but they are too big, and they even have gold paving up to their front doors.'

'These are the mansions I have prepared for those who love Me. Come, let me take you to yours... Follow Me!'

All of a sudden they had turned off on a path and there was a huge mansion before them. And although the front door was closed, they walked straight through it without it even opening.

Des was surprised by what he saw inside, for it was like taking a step back in history. He was in an old-fashioned kitchen with a kettle hanging over an open fire on the hearth, and some rustic wooden bunks in the corner.

Lit by a single candle, this simple one-roomed home seemed quite dark and dingy and the stone floor was cold and uninviting, yet Des knew his family was somehow connected to this place.

He could also see an antique loom where some kind of mat was being woven, and there were portraits of people hanging on the wall that seemed to resemble his family. 'How does this relate to me?' he thought to himself.

Then Des saw an open Bible, prominently displayed in the centre of the room and surrounded by an eternal flame, and as he looked at it, it became brighter and brighter like a ball of fire.

He had never seen anything like this before, yet there was a sense that this place belonged to him. 'Lord, where are we?' Des asked. 'Somehow this seems to have something to do with my inheritance.'

'Follow Me. You will understand more as we go further,' came the reply, and before Des knew it, he had passed through the walls into another time-frame and into a completely different home of another generation.

This house had no ceiling, as the roof was thatched, and there was a loft room and quite different furnishings, but one thing was the same – the Bible was wide open, and there was a large flame burning brightly in the centrefold.

Des followed the Lord from house to house, looking at the black-and-white family photographs on the walls, until finally he came to a house where he knew exactly where he was. Straight away he knew he was in his grandmother's home. She was a firm believer and he recognized her ever-open Bible on the table, almost as if it was her personal trademark.

'This is my grandmother's place!' Des exclaimed. 'Granny Huxford's house!'

'That's right, this is your family line. All these homes have belonged to your ancestors who have loved and served Me, and who are here with Me.'

Des looked around earnestly for family photos on the walls, but the only picture he could find was his grandmother's photo and his. 'Where are the pictures of my father and uncles?' he cried. 'Where are the pictures of my sisters and cousins?'

'They are not yet part of My Kingdom,' the Lord answered, 'and until they serve Me, their photographs cannot be here. But if they repent of their sin and give their lives to Me, then their pictures will be a part of this house.

'You have a great family inheritance,' the Lord continued. 'Many of your grandmother's family – of the Huxford line – were godly people and they served Me faithfully in preaching the Gospel. I want to introduce you to some of them.'

Des was amazed as many young people started coming up to him, dressed in beautiful clothes, without the slightest grey hair or trace of ageing. They were all beautiful, healthy and strong.

'This is your great, great, great grandfather – he served Me in Scotland,' Des heard the Lord say as he looked at his forefather, who appeared even younger than him! None of them talked, but there was instant communication between the Lord, Des and his ancestor. It was as if a very quick film clip of this man's life and what he went through for the Gospel was being played out. In an instant everything was revealed to Des in three-dimensional images that went through his mind like a movie.

It was so quick. In the twinkling of an eye, Des could see all the suffering his ancestor had endured for the Lord, and what a great man of faith he was. One by one, his relatives came and shared with him – but not his grandmother, who was still alive at the time.

'But how then can I be in her house, Lord?'

'I have prepared this place for her, for when her time comes,' the Lord Jesus replied. 'All of these people you have seen have completed their tasks on earth and they are now here with Me, where they are praying for you and cheering you on.

'Did I not tell you in My Word that I go and prepare a place for My people? Your grandmother's time is not yet up, but she will be coming soon and this is her place, and you have seen it.'

Des immediately recalled the words of Jesus in John 14:2:

In My Father's house are many mansions; if it were not so, I would have told you. I go to prepare a place for you.

'Did I not also tell you that I have surrounded you with such a cloud of witnesses?' the Lord continued. 'They are those you have seen today!'

Des's thoughts wandered to Hebrews 12:1–3, a favourite passage of Scripture. In fact, he could recite it word for word:

> *Therefore we also, since we are surrounded by so great a cloud of witnesses, let us lay aside every weight, and the sin which so easily ensnares us, and let us run with endurance the race that is set before us, looking unto Jesus, the author and finisher of our faith, who for the joy that was set before Him endured the cross, despising the shame, and has sat down at the right hand of the throne of God.*

'Wow!' thought Des, 'how great You are, Lord, that You would choose a sinner like me, and take my life and use it for Your glory. I will never give up on the race You have called me to run, and I will always look to You for my salvation and deliverance. For what Satan has meant for evil, I know You will turn around for good.'

God was to reveal much of what would happen to Des in his future ministry during this divine encounter, including many of the places the Lord would take him to in the years to come, such as Australia, the Philippines, Norway, Russia, Germany and various countries in Africa.

One minute Des and the Lord were flying through the air, and the next they were descending through the clouds. Des could hear the sound of several aeroplanes as the Australian scrubland materialized beneath them.

To the left there was a busy Air Force base, and Des could see fighter jets taking off and landing. To the right was a mountain, where a large church building was nestling at its base.

The next moment Des and the Lord were walking through the aisles, observing the congregation as they participated in the service. There were about 5,000 people gathered to listen to a white-haired old man who was preaching.

'We need to be much more sensitive to the Holy Spirit, if we are ever to see revival in this city,' he said, tears filling his eyes. 'I urge you to worship the Lord right now with all of your heart,' he challenged the crowd.

'Follow Me!' the Lord said, as He led Des through the pews. Every now and then, He stopped at a man or a woman and reached out His hand to impart something into their lives.

Des could see the Lord was crying as He knelt down to wash a man's feet with His tears, but the man's heart was hardened and he could not receive anything from the Lord.

This happened many times as Jesus walked through the whole church, trying to minister to the people, but very few actually received anything.

'Why is it Lord, that You were only able to minister to so few?' Des asked.

'Those that I was able to minister to, they serve Me whole-heartedly. The rest serve Me for their own gain and their own ambition, and I cannot do anything for them. Those who touch Me, I will touch. Those who don't touch Me, I can do nothing for.'

'I don't understand why You brought me here, Lord,' said Des respectfully.

'This is part of your destiny,' the Lord answered. 'I will bring you here to Australia to minister to these people. You have been praying and crying out for direction for the rest of your life, and I am now showing you your future.

'I spoke to you on a rubbish dump and told you things that you would do. And you have been faithful and believed what I told you. Now I am revealing the bigger picture to you, and I will take you from country to country and show you where you will serve Me, so that you will know where you are meant to be.'

'You are sending me to Australia, Lord?'

'Yes. I will bring you here, to this city, when you are ready, and you will be the pastor of this church. Now we must go, for I have more places I want to take you.'

And so the Lord took Des from country to country, revealing to him in part where his future ministry would take place.

God also allowed him to experience some of the horrors of hell, providing a shocking picture which motivates him to preach the Gospel more fervently each day – not out of fear but out of love and compassion.

The Lord also gave him a wonderful unique insight into what happens to the millions of babies who are aborted in the world today. All this and more is shared in later chapters, but for now, Des was still fighting for his very existence, even though the doctors of Hamilton ICU had long given up on him.

Back on the earth, Des's body lay lifeless, waiting for orderlies to take it to the hospital mortuary. The devil had come to destroy him outright, before his life became a further threat to the kingdom of darkness.

Satan and his demonic cohorts had unleashed a deadly illness upon Des, but God had preserved him and was about to raise him up from his deathbed, to continue serving the Lord with a powerful new conviction and a whole new lease of life.

'Now you must go back,' Jesus declared.

'But Lord, it has been too short, and there is still much I must learn. You are showing me all these things, and I need to learn more so that I don't make mistakes.'

'Get back in the boat. I have shown you things in part, but I will now show them to you in full through circumstances and the leading of My Spirit. And as you pray and you keep talking to Me, all these things will be revealed to you in due course.

'They will all come to pass, but I have shown you enough so that when you see these things, you will know it is Me and you will seek Me and pray for further direction, and I will lead you into the fulfilment of all these things. Now go!'

As a divine current took the boat briskly back across the crystal lake, Des was still coming to terms with the fact that he had to leave. 'I don't want to go back!' he shouted, looking down at the fish leading the vessel at a fast pace. 'Lord, don't leave me!'

'Do not worry!' came the thunderous response from the people on the shore, led by Peter, Paul, Elijah and Abraham, as they spoke in unison. 'You are not alone – you are surrounded by such a great cloud of witnesses. We are looking down upon you and we are cheering for you!'

The next minute Des felt he was falling head-first down a tunnel of light, and back into his physical body with a thump. He immediately woke up, throwing the sheet off his body to reveal his face.

The orderlies pushing his trolley screamed out in shock, quickly turning it around to get Des back to the ICU. Des was quite dazed as he came around, wondering what all the commotion was about.

As he looked at his arms, he realized how cold and blue his body was, and all of a sudden a doctor came running towards him. 'You're alive!' he shouted.

'Yes!' exclaimed Des, a little dumbfounded, as the medical team went into overdrive to warm him up and put him on a drip to replenish his fluids. Pretty soon he was reconnected to all the various monitors and undergoing multiple tests, but nothing appeared to be wrong with him.

'You were dead,' explained the doctor, almost disbelieving his own words. 'I have your death certificate. We were taking you through to the mortuary. You were dead for thirty-five minutes.'

'What was the matter with me?' Des asked.

'We don't know. We have no medical explanation for why you died. But you are alive now, and we can't see anything wrong with you!'

As he was leaving the hospital to go home, Des raised his hands in thanksgiving to the Father: 'Thank you, Lord, for healing me. Thank you, Lord, for preserving my life. Thank you, Lord Jesus, for turning a hopeless situation around. Instead of me dying, you have given me a blueprint for living! Death, where is your sting, where is your victory?'

Chapter 6

What Will You Die For?

'Are you prepared to die for the truth or will you deny Me?'

'If you speak against these men, they will kill you,' Des's long-time friend Yaw advised him, with tears streaming down his face. 'Don't do it,' he pleaded. 'They have the money to pay assassins to hunt you down and kill you. You will go home in a coffin. There is no way you will leave Ghana alive. Please don't do this. It is not your problem. I am pleading with you!'

Des listened to the words carefully. What was he to do? Should he take the advice of the man with whom he had ministered so many times in the past, or should he follow the conviction of his heart? Or should he perhaps reach a compromise? Once again he was in a life-and-death dilemma in West Africa, but now an even more sinister plot was brewing against him.

This time it was not to come from another religion, but from fellow believers, including Yaw, who had lived with Ros and Des in their home for six months when they were still in New Zealand. Now a high-ranking bishop in Ghana, Yaw had been a key part of Des and Ros's inspiration to come to Africa, and Des loved him like his own brother.

Unfortunately, this anointed man of God, who had been used so mightily by the Lord, had become involved with a band of false prophets who were literally holding the city of Kumasi to ransom.

Obviously still fuming about an entire Muslim community turning to Christ, the devil was going to do his best to wipe Des out. He was already controlling the Christian community in Kumasi through these false prophets and was not going to give up his hold on the people easily.

But would Des be the man for the job? Or would he decline to take up the assignment in fear for his life and the well-being of his wife back home? Facing witchcraft and sorcery head on is no walk in the park, especially when your opponents claim to be your brothers in the Lord.

While ministering in Accra, the capital of Ghana, Des had been invited by Bishop Yaw to visit him in Kumasi and meet a number of fellow prophets, but while he was on the way to the Sheraton Hotel for this meeting, the Lord's still voice began to whisper to Des:

'I am going to bring men around you who are false,' said the Lord. 'They proclaim My name but they serve the devil, operating in sorcery and witchcraft. Do not trust them or believe what they say. They are of the evil one.'

Des was immediately concerned, uncertain where this trip was taking him, but he loved Kumasi, especially the vibrant marketplace with its people from different nations coming to trade, and he was excited to be able to visit the city again.

'Anyway, it will be good to see Yaw again,' Des thought to himself, remembering the days when they had ministered together while Yaw was attending Faith Bible College in New Zealand.

'These men are prophets like you have never seen,' Yaw had told Des, 'and they want to meet you!'

Arriving in the hotel dining room, Des had every reason to be impressed by the twelve men sitting around the table. They were all wearing the finest Italian suits with immaculate leather shoes, Rolex watches and an abundance of gold jewellery. They had brand new Mercedes Benz cars in the car park and were dripping with money.

'*Akwaba!*' came the traditional welcome from the group of men as Des walked up to them.

'We're the prophets of this city,' one of the men told Des. 'God has given us the authority over Kumasi. We are the Lord's anointed here and we rule.'

'But how does that line up with the Word of God?' Des asked. 'Hasn't God given His authority to the body of Christ? I believe the Church is the foundation of all authority in the world, in a nation and in a city, but you are saying that you, as individual prophets, have all authority. I don't see that in Scripture,' Des continued. 'True prophets are messengers of God, sent to encourage the body, but they do not have authority over the body. Jesus Christ is the authority over the body. He is the Head of the Church and no other. Prophets are simply servants of Christ.'

At this stage the men around the table were clearly aggravated by Des's comments, but were trying to remain cordial. 'We are prophets of God – don't you believe that? If you were a true prophet of God, you would know this and give us due respect.'

'You may think you are men of God, but I believe you are playing around with some things that are not right.'

'Well, we will prove to you that we are of God by telling you some things that no other man of God has ever told you.'

'Okay,' Des replied. 'Let's see!'

One by one the 'prophets' started 'prophesying' – telling Des his mother's maiden name, how he was booted out of home and found Jesus on a rubbish dump, and all kinds of accurate information in detail: flight numbers, where he had been ministering, names of relatives, his wife's name and date of birth.

By the time all twelve had finished, it was as if every part of Des's life had been revealed, as well as key things that God had shown him. 'Is this not the truth?' the leader of the prophets asked smugly.

'Yes, everything you have said is true,' said Des. 'But what determines whether a person is a prophet of the Lord is the fruit of the Spirit in your life, and I see very little of that fruit in your lives.' (See Galatians 5:22–23.)

Des continued: 'Without that fruit, the gifts of the prophetic mantle are dangerous. If you don't have the maturity, and the character of God and the fruit of the Spirit, then your prophetic gifts can be used by the devil, because you do not have the integrity to carry the gift that is upon you.'

'Well, come with us now to one of our meetings,' they replied, 'and you will see for yourself the hand of God at work!'

Des was taken to a large warehouse-type building where a large crowd of people were singing songs accompanied by loud African drums. One of the prophets took the microphone and started calling people out so that he could 'prophesy' over them, but each of his prophecies had financial conditions attached. People receiving so-called 'words from the Lord' were told to provide specific amounts of money and do such and such before certain curses could be broken over their lives, and if they didn't do this within the specified time, they would have to face the consequences.

Des couldn't believe the demands the prophets were making on the people. It was blatant extortion, based on fear of the destruction that would come upon them and their families if they did not do everything the 'prophets' said. This was not prophetic ministry of the Holy Ghost; these men wanted payment for the gifts of God.

'Lord, you have confirmed to me that these men are wrong,' Des prayed under his breath. 'Their work is clearly of the devil – this is not the Spirit of the Lord, but a spirit of sorcery and bondage,' he thought as a righteous anger came upon him.

But as he began to reason, Des remembered he was in a foreign land, with a different culture. Who was he to judge? 'Let me not be judgmental,' he thought. 'I'll just watch.'

Just then, a woman's name was called out. She was hiding at the back of the crowd, but she eventually came running out, obviously quite pregnant.

'Where is my money?' the 'prophet' shouted, grabbing her by the hair. 'I prophesied over you last week and told you that God showed me that you must get me $2,500 and that you had a week to bring it. Where is my money?

'I told you, that if you brought me the money, then God would stop the affair your husband is having with another woman, and turn your husband's heart back to God and back to you...

'But you haven't come up with the money, and now God is going to allow your husband to be infected by HIV/AIDS, and he is going to become violent and come after you and beat you and take everything you have. Where is my money?' the 'prophet' screamed.

The woman began to plead with the man: 'Have

mercy on me! Please don't allow this to come upon me. It is true, I found out that my husband is having an affair, and I have been trying to get the money. I even sold my body in prostitution to try to raise the funds for you, but I am also worried about my baby...'

She had about 800 dollars with her, but it wasn't enough. The man with the microphone grabbed her and started pulling her around the stage as she screamed, crying out for mercy.

'This is what happens when you do not honour the Man of God,' he shouted, taking the woman's money and putting it in his pocket. 'This woman has stolen from God and robbed me. Now God's hand of vengeance is upon her.'

Des looked at the bishop. 'Yaw, are you going to do something about this or am I?' he asked.

At that Yaw ran up to the man and told him to let the woman go. 'Calm down, calm down! We don't want to upset our friend!'

'Ah, we have a prophet all the way from New Zealand here with us,' the 'prophet' said, remembering his guest and moving to hand Des the microphone. 'Prophesy, prophet – we want to hear what you have to say!'

'No, thank you,' Des replied. 'God has not given me a word to bring right now.'

'Come on, this is not the West. This is where prophets are honoured for the gifts they have. You will get paid. We will share a percentage of the offerings we have received,' pointing to a large wooden barrel in the centre of the auditorium, where people were running to put their money in, as well as their watches and other jewellery.

Then he walked over to the container to see how full it was. 'God will only answer your prayer as you put in your gift,' he told the crowd. Manipulating them, he said they had to bring an offering to secure their breakthrough.

'Prophesy, prophet,' he challenged Des again.

Des looked at him straight. 'The day I prophesy for money is the day I go to hell,' Des said. 'It is the day I lose my salvation. You cannot buy the gifts of God. You don't have the gift of God, you have bought your gift from the devil. Get behind me, Satan!'

'How dare you!' the man said as the crowd began to talk loudly among themselves. 'Who do you think you are? You don't understand this culture. This is how it has been done here for generations. God is with –'

'In the name of Jesus Christ I rebuke that spirit of sorcery over you! I muzzle your false gift in the name of Jesus!' Des proclaimed with a voice of authority.

The man hit the deck and started squirming on the floor.

'Now leave!'

The false prophet got up and started to move towards the door.

'Yaw, can you show me anywhere in the Word where the gifts of God are there to bring people into bondage, put curses on them and take from God's people? But you know there is no such Scripture reference,' Des said to his friend in front of the congregation. 'You know that this ministry that you are involved in is for the glory of man and is of the devil, because it only brings bondage. See this man – his gift has left him now!'

'It's not like that,' the bishop replied, trying to calm things down. 'He really is a man of God. Let him continue prophesying. We have come here to minister to the people – let's not let them down.'

But when the man tried to prophesy again, he couldn't say a word.

After this extraordinary service, the local pastors in

Kumasi were astounded by Des's bravery and arranged to meet with him a few days later.

'These prophets have had a major stronghold over this city for many years. They are very wicked and have great power over the people because the people are so afraid of them,' one of the pastors confided with Des at a hastily called church leaders' meeting. 'We have tried to stand against them and mobilize our congregation in prayer,' said another pastor, 'but they just laughed at us.'

The full extent of this evil regime became apparent as the pastors shared, one by one.

'I went and confronted the "prophets" and told them to stay away from my people,' another pastor lamented, 'but it was useless. They threatened me and told me that my daughter would develop a fever and die.

'When this happened as they said, we prayed for her but nothing happened. We took her to the doctor, but he couldn't do anything for her, and she died.

'I could have gone to them and retracted and paid them money, and maybe my daughter would still be alive, but I could not do that. I couldn't go and proclaim that they were of God, when I knew the evil power they were operating under.'

Des had heard enough. 'But why have you brought me here?' he asked. 'You are the spiritual authority over this city. God has given you the responsibility to address this issue. Why do you want me here?'

'Because you rebuked one of the "prophets" and the evil spirit within him left him immediately. Please help us! We will bring all our churches together and you can speak to them. Our people have heard this report and they will listen to you. Please teach us about the true ministry of a prophet and how the prophetic gifts should operate.'

Bishop Yaw, who was in the meeting with Des, motioned for him to follow him outside. 'We need to stop right here. Come outside and let's talk about this. Don't do this!' he said with tears in his eyes. 'If you say anything further against these men and convince the people they are false, so that they are no longer bowed down to, they will kill you.

'This is their livelihood, and their reputation. If the people turn against them, they will be treated like lepers in our culture. If you speak against them, they have the money to pay assassins to hunt you down. You will go home in a coffin. There is no way you will leave Ghana alive. Please don't do this – it is not your problem,' he pleaded.

'When I returned from New Zealand, I tried to address these men and tell them what was wrong, but they even overpowered me. Yes, I am associated with them, but I don't want you to die. You're an evangelist. You are here to do crusades. Keep on preaching the Gospel, but leave this well alone. Go home alive, and you'll be welcome to come back.'

Des remembers the conflict that was going on in his mind at the time. Here was a man whom he really looked up to, who had been used by God to work some incredible miracles in the past – and maybe he was right.

'Maybe this isn't my problem. Why should I get involved?' Des thought as a battle raged in his head. 'That's right – I am an evangelist, and I don't want any trouble. This is all church politics and has nothing to do with me!'

At that moment, the Lord spoke. This time it was not the still, small voice that Des knew so well. This time it was loud and clear and very direct, silencing Yaw's voice in Des's ears as the bishop continued to ramble on, trying to persuade him to take his advice.

'What do you believe, Des?' the Lord asked.

'You know I believe in You,' Des replied.

'That is not what I asked you,' the Lord answered. 'Do you believe these men are from Me and are here to build up the body, or do you believe they are of the devil?'

'Well, I believe they are of the devil – there is no doubt about it. Everything I have seen is of Satan. You came to set the captives free, and yet these men are holding people captive. That is not of You.'

'You are right. So why won't you stand on what you believe, and speak the truth?'

'But Lord, if I do, my life will be in danger. Can't You handle this in another way?'

'Des, it doesn't matter when you die. Whether you die today, tomorrow or many years from now, it doesn't matter. All that matters to Me is what you are prepared to die for.

'Will you die for truth or will you compromise truth? What is it worth if a man gains the whole world and loses his own soul? Are you prepared to die for truth? For I am the truth. Or will you deny Me?'

This was one of the most profound things the Lord had ever said to Des, and he realized just how wicked his heart really was.

'You're right, Lord. I am trying to manipulate Scripture so I can walk away from this, and I am prepared to compromise the truth and leave the Church suffering in bondage to the devil. And by refusing to take responsibility, I am denying my Lord Jesus Christ and saying my life is more valuable than His life.

'Lord, forgive me – my heart is full of compromise. You're right, Lord – it doesn't matter when I die or how I die. All that matters is what I am dying for.'

As this conversation with the Lord came to an end, Des blurted out his definitive answer to his friend. 'Yaw, *I will speak!*'

'Then you will die,' the bishop repeated.

Chapter 7

I'm a Dead Man!

GHANA

'Alive to Christ and dead to myself – you cannot kill a dead man.'

'God is with me,' Des tried to assure the Ghanaian church leaders and the bodyguards they had provided. 'You're panicking for nothing! Nobody is going to kill me.

'The Lord has told me to speak the truth, no matter what. And if I die here in Ghana, then at least I have died obedient to the Lord. Whether I live or die is God's choice, not mine. I will leave that up to Him.'

And having confessed this, a great peace came to rest upon him. He now had a deep awareness that his life was not his own. He had been bought with a great price, as he had read so often in Corinthians:

> *Do you not know that your body is the Temple of the Holy Ghost, whom you received from God? You are not your own, but rather you were bought at a price.*
>
> 1 Corinthians 6:19–20

Des remembered that he had surrendered his spirit, body and soul to God. He had to be willing to lay down his earthly

94

life for the Father. He had to be prepared to lay aside his will and yield to the Father's will.

'This was one of the most liberating revelations in my life,' he recalls. 'When we come to Christ, we belong to Him and our lives are completely within His hands.'

And so about 20,000 people gathered to hear Des speak. The place was packed.

Then the twelve false prophets came in and sat down in the front row. As they walked in, the people bowed to them and started throwing money at their feet, as was their custom.

Des cried out to God in desperation: 'Lord, I am solely dependent upon you. I don't know what to say. You have to move – otherwise I am a dead man.'

He began to preach one of the most powerful messages he had ever delivered, and the anointing on the meeting was tangible. He explained to the crowd about the nature of the gifts of the Holy Spirit, and started to call people up and prophesy over them as a practical illustration of what he had been saying.

Then he asked a man to stand up, along with the false prophet who had prophesied over him. 'Sir, did this man not come to you on this date and tell you this and this and this?' Des said, recalling all the details. 'Tell me publicly – am I right?'

'Yes, he did,' came the answer.

'But he is a liar,' Des answered, 'because this is in fact what happened.' Des put the record straight with a number of facts and figures.

And so the Lord used an authentic demonstration of the revelation gifts to discredit the false prophets seated on the front row, revealing to the people that they were blinded by fear and what they had experienced with these men was a counterfeit prophetic ability in operation.

'You must repent,' Des challenged the crowd. 'The reason why these men and the devil have authority over you is because you have bowed to them out of fear and have neglected God in the process. This is idolatry and it is a sin, and you need to repent.'

When the false prophets realized they had overstayed their welcome, as the crowd started to turn against them, they began to make for the front exit.

But Des was not finished with them, and called them back to confront them directly and give them an opportunity to repent of their wickedness. He told them that God still loved them, that despite the fact that they had come under a spirit of sorcery, if they repented before the Lord, He would forgive them and deliver them from their deception.

He also shared with them that God had a plan and purpose for their lives, and His mercy would be upon them, if they would only repent. And if they did, then the Lord would restore them, and no harm would come to them.

Two of the men started to shake uncontrollably and were clearly convicted, but none of them came forward... until a while later, when one of them came running back. He shouted something out in his native language to the pastors.

'We have to get you out of here quickly!' one of the pastors told Des. 'They have already put a bounty on your head. The word is out and there will be armed guerrilla soldiers coming after you.'

'There's a bounty on my head?' Des stuttered. 'How much am I worth?'

'The bounty is 5,000 dollars for the man who shoots you and 25,000 for your body, when it is brought to them. We have to get you out of here immediately!'

Here in Kumasi it wasn't uncommon for pastors to have several bodyguards to protect them and their congregations from radical Muslim snipers, who would try to disrupt their church services. In Kumasi there was no shortage of weapons, and hired killers were freely available to knock anybody off for the right price.

Des was hastily taken out of the meeting as the capacity crowd began to disperse. He and Yaw were seated with a bodyguard in the back of the bishop's Mercedes, while the driver raced through the streets of Kumasi to find a safe house, followed by another car full of bodyguards.

Des could see the worried look on the driver's face in the rear-view mirror. The bishop and the bodyguards were also clearly stressed by the whole situation.

'Turn left here,' Yaw instructed the driver, 'now right...' And so the directions continued until they pulled up at a large double-storey house surrounded by a high fence. The two cars pulled into the driveway and the gates were immediately locked behind them.

'Why are you so worried?' Des said to Yaw as they were quickly taken inside. 'They are not going to find us here. God is with us. Let's go to bed.'

But the bishop knew better. He instructed some of the guards to go out into the neighbourhood and ask the street kids to alert them if they heard anyone coming towards 'the compound'.

At that time, Des's knowledge of West Africa was still quite limited, despite the fact that his hosts in Burkina Faso had been slaughtered in front of him some eight months before, when he had been taken prisoner.

Tonight he was full of faith, but really he had no idea of the extent of the threat to him and his hosts, and he went to sleep quite oblivious to what they were up against.

Then, in the middle of the night, a boy came running into the compound, yelling at the top of his voice. 'We have to leave at once,' a bodyguard instructed Des and Yaw, leading them down the stairs to get them into the car parked outside.

But it was too late. All of a sudden gunshots could be heard across the compound. 'We have to get you out of here!' another bodyguard whispered. 'Otherwise we'll all be dead – it's our only chance.'

Some of the guards managed to get Yaw into the car while others returned fire. Now four bodyguards surrounded Des as they took him towards the vehicle.

In the moonlight he could see that the rear window of the Mercedes had been shot out. There were bits of shattered glass everywhere and bullet holes all over the back of the car.

'I'm a dead man!' The thought went through Des's mind like lightning as he ran towards the car. One by one the four bodyguards fell to the ground. Snipers had shot them dead from a rooftop across the road, but somehow Des was still standing.

'Lord, help me!' Des cried out, raising his hands. 'Enable me to overcome the devil that is trying to kill me. Lord, I thank You for the prophecies over my life which have not yet been fulfilled. Thank You for the destiny You have given me. Show the devil You haven't finished with me yet!' he proclaimed.

'The devil has no authority over me because I have not finished the work that You have set before me,' continued Des, confessing the promises of God. *'Get behind me, Satan!'* he shouted.

He continued to raise his hands and pray as everything went quiet. Then all of a sudden, Des felt something grab him and push him down as the snipers opened fire again. It was like a big hand came down on his head and threw him to the ground.

Bullets were flying all around him, and it seemed to go on forever as Des heard the sound of bullets bouncing off the brick building. But then there was complete silence...

Des remembers lying on the ground wondering whether or not he was still alive. He moved his arms and legs to see if his body was still intact and felt his clothes in case he was bleeding.

'I must have a couple of bullets in me at least,' he thought, but there was no blood. Miraculously, he had not been hit.

But as he sat up, there at his feet was a pile of bullets. 'What's going on?' he asked himself as he stumbled to his feet. 'Is Yaw okay?' he thought, running to the car. 'Is he still alive?'

As Des approached the Mercedes he could hear the bishop praying: 'God, forgive me,' he sobbed. 'I am guilty of robbing from the Church... I am guilty of...' And he continued to list his sins, seemingly unaware of what was going on around him.

Des turned around as he heard footsteps behind him. He could see a group of men walking towards him from the other side of the road.

'Now they are going to come and blow us away,' Des thought, as he saw their camouflage uniforms in the moonlight.

But as soon as the soldiers entered the compound, they dropped their weapons to the ground and knelt before Des.

'Please forgive us!' they cried.

'Don't allow your God to punish us,' said one.

'What must we do to be right with your God?' asked another.

'Hold on – what do you mean?' Des asked. 'Explain to me what happened.'

'We are the ones who were on the roof shooting. We killed your bodyguards and we were going to kill you, but when we started firing, we saw the tallest man we have ever seen, shining like the sun,' explained one of the soldiers.

'The man was so bright, he blinded us so that we could not see you or where we were aiming. Then as we shot at you, he stood in front of you and caught the bullets with his bare hands and placed them at your feet. Can't you see them over there?'

Des had seen the bullets, but what had happened was only now beginning to register as he looked at the pile of used ammunition where he had been lying on the ground.

'We know your God is the true God,' said another soldier. 'We know that He is with you because He has stopped you from dying. Death has no power over you – you cannot be killed, you cannot die. How can we serve your God?'

One by one, Des led each of the men to the Lord, kneeling down with them and praying the sinner's prayer. Once again, God had sovereignly intervened in his life – and as the Lord always does, He was going to get double mileage out of the situation.

Not only had the lives of a young evangelist and a rather wayward bishop been saved, but a whole group of hired guns had repented and given their lives to the Lord. Many of them are now in the ministry themselves.

'A number of those men are pastors today,' Des recalls. 'They were so convicted by what happened, and overcome by the power of God.'

Des had experienced another amazing miracle, but he was not out of danger yet. The local pastors were overjoyed to hear this extraordinary testimony but continued to tell Des that it would be best if he left Kumasi post-haste.

'God is with you,' said Pastor Emmanuel, remembering how the Lord had delivered them both from the dead man's family, and marvelling at this latest miraculous escape.

'I agree,' said Pastor Kofi from another church in Kumasi. 'We have to get you to Accra, until God has dealt with the false prophets and things have cooled down.' (When Des had confronted the 'prophets' the night before, he had told them that the Lord had given them twenty-four hours to repent and get right with Him, and if they didn't, then God's hand of judgment would come upon them.)

'We don't need to worry about the false prophets any more – already two are dead,' said another pastor. 'But we have to get you out of here because there is still a price on your head, and every man in Kumasi who can lay hold of a gun wants to kill you. But first we must take you to the King, because he has heard the story and he wants to meet with you and offer you his hand of protection.'

And so Des once again had an audience with King Otumfuo, who had helped him previously. This time, in order to afford him his royal protection, the King gave Des a set of elaborate robes and another set for Ros back home (see photo section), signifying that the wearer was associated with the royal family, and if they were harmed in any way, the perpetrator was taking on the full might of the King.

'Wear these,' the King decreed. 'If you wear these, no man will touch you. They know what it means. If they hurt you in any way, it is a declaration of war on me.'

Des put the clothes on and the pastors arranged a vehicle for him to travel in that night under the cover of darkness. Yaw accompanied him, ensuring that they took all the back roads to Accra, but as they were entering the city, their car was stopped at a roadblock.

'Isn't this the man we are looking for?' a soldier asked his colleague.

The bishop courageously got out of the car to negotiate with the men.

After a few minutes of heated discussion and some obvious bargaining, he got back into his seat. 'We're fine,' he said. 'I've paid them. They've got more than they would have from the "prophets" and they're happy to let you go. Let's head for the airport.'

Just then one of the soldiers knocked on Des's window. 'I want to thank you for praying for my daughter,' he said. 'My wife and I brought her to your crusade in Accra. She was born deformed, but after you prayed she was made whole...

'I am sorry we have to take the money. I am a Christian and hold nothing personal against you. We are just doing our jobs.'

Des could hardly believe what the man was saying. How could he do such a thing, and call himself a Christian?

But he was free to go, and they finally made it to the airport, where corrupt officials could have made further demands on Des, but wearing his royal robes, he was able to clear emigration formalities quickly and board the plane.

'All in all, this was a hair-raising but faith-building experience,' Des recalls. 'But the most important thing was that the Lord showed me that my heart was full of compromise. He revealed to me that I was prepared to adjust the truth to my liking and I wasn't prepared to lay down my life for what I believed in.

'I also learnt that in times of intense opposition, when our lives are on the line, that is the time when we need to raise our hands to God and praise Him. When all odds are against us, that is when we need to humble ourselves and cry out to God and say, "Lord, help me! I can't do this on my own. Empower me to stand for you and set me free from the enemy."

'Because I raised my hands and cried out to God and proclaimed His promises, the Lord delivered me, because there is power in the tongue and the Lord is committed to what we confess. When I humbled myself, and asked God to deliver me from the hand of the enemy, so that I could be faithful to fulfil all the things He had laid before me, that was when I saw the hand of God come down and deliver me.'

Des Sinclair's near encounters with death and the miraculous escapes he has experienced seem to set him apart as someone uniquely used by God, but the truth is that God is not a respecter of persons, and the same grace is available to all who would believe.

Chapter 8

Pressing on Towards the Mark

*'How do you recover from something like this?
With guilt and greif choking the life out of you?'*

'Come to the hospital right away!' came the hysterical cry. 'It's Karin – she has been beaten up and they can't stop the bleeding.'

The words shot through the pastor's heart like a lightning bolt. The phone had awakened him from a deep sleep. Was he dreaming? How could this have happened to his fiancée?

'What happened last night, Des?' Karin's mother asked, her voice trailing off in between sobs. 'Didn't you see Karin into the house when you brought her home?'

It was a question that had the potential to derail him with guilt for the rest of his life and completely destroy his ministry. Here he was, the leader of a large congregational church in Australia, at the tender age of nineteen, and yet everything was now falling apart.

Despite the fact that God had clearly called Des to Australia, and had even shown him a picture of the church he would pastor, it would still prove to be one of the most difficult assignments of his life, and it was only by the grace of God that he would ever recover.

Following Des's near-fatal experience in Hamilton, his heart had begun to burn with a passion to minister in Australia, New Zealand's closest neighbour across the sea. But he was unaware that the men who had taken him under their wing would not easily support the idea.

When the elders of his church in Tokoroa asked Des what he had planned for the next year, Des shared with them that he felt that the Lord was leading him to Australia, but they were not convinced.

'We're not sure you are hearing God's timing on this,' the pastor told the excited young evangelist, who was all too eager to pack his bags. 'We feel you should at least do a full-time Bible course first. Then, once you have done that, we will ordain you and look at giving you your first church.'

'You first have to prove yourself with a small church,' cautioned another elder, 'working your way up, step by step. Then maybe in twenty years' time, you may be ready to handle the larger church in Aussie you have spoken about.'

Des walked away from this conversation feeling really frustrated. 'These men are against me,' he cried out to the Lord. 'They don't understand what you have called me to do.'

'My Word is very clear,' the Lord answered. 'Younger men must learn from the older men in the faith and submit to them,' he reminded the young preacher. 'Submit to them and I will soften their hearts, and I will get you to where you should be!'

Even though Des felt he was right, and in his heart he wanted to rebel, he realized his attitude was wrong and began to repent of having an independent spirit. 'Okay, whatever you say I should do, I will do it,' he later told the elders, who were pleased that he was prepared to submit to their leadership.

A few months later, during the Christmas holidays, one of the pastors who was overseeing Des's ministry training bumped into one of his former youth leaders, a young man named Dennis. He had moved to Northern Queensland, but was over in New Zealand visiting his family.

A hunter and a taxidermist, Dennis was out in the bush much of the time, where he was able to minister effectively to Australia's Aboriginal people.

'How is that young fellow who started the church on the rubbish dump?' Dennis asked the pastor, remembering the times when he had ministered along with Des in Levin.

'He's doing well,' the pastor answered. 'Funnily enough, he believes God is calling him up north!'

'Well, why don't you send him up to me? Let him come and minister to the Aborigines with me. Maybe God is calling him. Let him come for a couple of months, then maybe he can go down south and get involved in a church there.'

Just after Christmas, the elders called a meeting to tell Des that they had decided he could go to Australia after all. 'We have been praying about this, and have talked to Dennis, and we have decided that yes, you can go to Aussie.

'You will spend three months with him in Northern Queensland, then perhaps you can go down to Melbourne and work in the youth ministry there, and when you come back we will ordain you, and give you your own church in New Zealand.'

Des was overjoyed! Now he could move on with what God had called him to do, with the full blessing of those whom the Lord had set up in authority over him.

As soon as Des arrived in Northern Queensland, he knew this was exactly where he was meant to be. There was one snag, however. Dennis was nowhere to be seen at the airport, and Des could not reach him on the number he had been given. He had been waiting in the arrivals hall for a number of hours and it was now after midnight. Dennis had obviously 'gone walkabout' – the Aboriginal term for going away without telling anyone! Perhaps he was on a hunting trip and the church had not been able to get through to him to make proper arrangements for Des to be fetched. All Des knew was that it was late, and he was tired.

The next moment a man came up to him. 'Good day, Des. How're you doing?'

Des didn't recognize the man, but he thought Dennis must have sent him.

'I'm a bit frustrated!' he replied. 'Dennis was meant to pick me up ages ago, and I don't have enough money for a hotel...'

'It doesn't matter, mate – you'll see Dennis tomorrow. Come with me. There's a backpackers' hostel down the road where you can get a good night's sleep.'

The next morning, when Des woke up in the dormitory, his new-found friend had vanished. 'Where's the guy I came in with last night?' he asked the three Swiss backpackers he was sharing with.

'What do you mean?' they replied. 'We saw you both come in, but then you went to sleep straight away and he left.'

As Des was leaving, he checked the register from the night before, but the place in the book where he had watched the man fill in his details was now completely blank.

'It must have been an angel,' he thought to himself, finally realizing what had happened, and marvelling at God's provision in this situation. He was further encouraged that the heavenly messenger had told him he wouldn't have any problem tracking Dennis down during the course of the day.

As he was passing an information centre, Des felt the Lord prompting him to ask the woman behind the counter to help him get in touch with Dennis. He felt a little stupid, and wondered if he had heard right, but the Lord had already intervened in a supernatural way, and he did not want to be disobedient.

'Excuse me – this may sound weird, but do you know a guy called Dennis from New Zealand? He's a taxidermist.'

'How on earth would I know? There are thousands of people living in this city!' the woman said, looking at him strangely, as if to say, 'That's not quite the kind of information I offer!'

'Thanks anyway,' Des said, turning around to walk away.

'Hey, wait a minute,' the woman said. 'I think my son-in-law may know a Kiwi guy like that. Let me just ring him to find out.'

Sure enough, the woman got Des another number for Dennis and he was able to make contact.

'Dennis, where are you?' Des asked. 'I was expecting you to meet me at the airport.'

'Sorry, I understood you were arriving on another day,' Dennis answered. 'I'll come through and pick you up now!'

Thankfully, it wasn't too long before the two men were heading into the city in Dennis's old Chevy.

'There is a church here,' Des said to Dennis. 'It's near an Air Force base and a mountain. Can we check it out?'

'Yeah, sure. There's a youth-oriented church around here, I think. I'm sure I'll be able to find it. I'll try to take you there now.'

As they drove closer to the mountain, Des began to recognize the terrain and started to give Dennis directions. 'Turn left here…' he instructed.

'How do you know? Have you been here before?'

'Yeah, I have!' Des answered. 'You remember what I told you about that time I died, and went to heaven? Well, the Lord brought me to this place during that experience.'

Dennis was amazed. 'Well, it looks like we have come at the right time. It seems there is a service going on,' he said.

Tears filled Des's eyes as he stood at the back of the church, just as he had done with the Lord, and he knew that he was in the very centre of God's will for his life.

The two men sat down and listened to the rest of the message that the elderly pastor was sharing. Immediately after the service ended, Des went up to the front to speak to him.

'You have been praying for God to send you help, and the Lord has brought me here,' Des said to the pastor. 'I'm here to serve you. Tell me what I must do.'

The old man looked at Des, a little bit dumbfounded. 'It's funny you say that. You know, I am eighty-years-old and my retirement is long overdue, so we have indeed been praying for a new pastor.

'In fact, God has shown us very clearly who is to replace me. The church has received a number of prophetic words that a young man would walk up to me and boldly declare that God had sent him to get involved here, that he would be from New Zealand, and he would be very young. Are you the one?'

'Yes, I am,' Des answered in his give-away Kiwi accent.

'God also told me that the young man had been here before... Have you been here before?'

'Not physically,' Des answered. 'You may think I'm crazy, but yes, I have been here before with my Lord, and I walked with Him among the people as He reached out to touch them.'

The old pastor was filled with emotion and began to cry. 'Then you'd better come and see me tomorrow,' he said.

The following day, Des met with the pastor and they had a wonderful time of sharing together in the Lord.

'I'll tell you what,' the pastor said. 'We have a special youth service this Sunday evening. Why don't you preach, so we can see what you're made of, and whether you're the one God is sending us.'

Des, of course, was eager to take up the challenge, and the Lord moved sovereignly in the meeting. Not surprisingly, they kept on asking him back, and the more he preached, the more involved he became in the leadership of the church.

Then, before he knew it, Des had been ordained at the unheard-of age of eighteen and had taken over as pastor of the United Church, made up primarily of Presbyterians and Methodists.

This was a ministry which was just coming into the move of the Spirit, and was ripe for the young, dynamic preacher, who revolutionized just about everything. When Des took over the church already had a large congregation, and in less than a year and a half, its membership tripled in size.

'We lost a lot of people in the beginning,' Des remembers, 'folk who weren't happy with my new approach to the things of the Spirit. But after that, the Lord moved mightily and the church grew quickly, despite the fact that it was my first official church and I made many mistakes. But I certainly learnt a lot.

'When I first started, I was too vision-focused and determined to fulfil that vision at any cost. I looked upon people as being there to fulfil my dreams. You could even say that my style of leadership was dictatorial, in a sense. My philosophy was that I was there to equip people to do something for the Lord, and I wasn't really interested in their problems.'

Des was entirely focused on street evangelism and reaching out to the needy in the inner city. The Lord continued to bless Des's ministry, but He clearly had to change the young pastor's heart.

At the beginning of the new year, during the church's annual period of prayer and fasting, the Lord began to speak clearly to Des as he gathered with his leaders.

'The church was growing so rapidly that we didn't have enough leaders,' Des recalls, 'and I was so demanding that the leaders I did have didn't want to stick around for long. I kept on praying and binding the devil from stealing my leaders, but then the Lord showed me that if I couldn't get people to serve, it was not their fault, but mine.'

Des was on the twentieth day of a forty-day fast when he started to pray for the situation in earnest. 'Lord, I am so tired of the way Satan keeps stealing my leaders. The church cannot grow unless people are prepared to serve.'

'Des, why do you give the devil so much credit?' the Lord asked. 'He may be doing a good job at causing your leaders to resign, but you're doing a better one.'

That got Des's attention. 'But, Lord, I am doing everything I can in your name. What do you mean?'

'Yes, you are building a vision, but it's not Mine. You're

building your own vision and the devil has every right to attack you in this way. You are called to lead My people to fulfil the vision that I have laid before this church, but you are way ahead of the people, and you are dictating to them how they must catch up with you.

'You only see them as a means to fulfil your vision, but My heart is for the people. You have lost My heart for the people. You need to inspire them and walk with them to fulfil the vision, not push them when they are miles behind you.

'You are so opinionated, and when people challenge you on anything, you treat them as if they are the ones in rebellion. You are scattering My sheep, and woe unto those who scatter My flock. You have lost sight of who I am.'

Once again, Des had to repent and change his ways, and start leading the church in the way that the Lord had instructed. Pretty soon there was a complete turnaround in the leadership deficit, as the Lord began to raise up new leaders to cope with the growth. Then, just as everything seemed to be blossoming, disaster struck.

Des had fallen in love with a young woman by the name of Karin. They weren't trying to make anything happen, but had begun to develop a friendship, with the blessing of the elders, and were now engaged.

At the time, the church was holding evangelistic youth rallies every Saturday night in the city centre, and afterwards Des was responsible for taking Karin and a number of his young assistants home.

That fateful night, he had finished preaching rather late and it was already well after eleven o'clock when he pulled up to his fiancée's family home. Even so, the lights inside the house were still on.

'I'll just run in on my own,' Karin said as Des opened

his door to get out of the vehicle. 'It's late and you still have to drop everyone off – I'll be fine. Look, my parents are home and my brother's bedroom light is on.'

Something inside of Des prompted him to take the time to see her in: 'Don't let her go into the house alone – there is nobody home,' was the thought that came into his mind, but he quickly brushed it aside as he saw her parents' car in the drive.

'Off you go, Des – you have to be up early tomorrow morning to preach. I'll see you at church. Goodnight, love...' Karin said as she ran inside. They were the last words he would ever hear her speak.

'Foolishly, I listened to man and not to God,' Des recalls today. 'I should have taken her in – it would have only taken a few more minutes – but I didn't. Instead I took the others home and jumped into bed as quickly as I could.'

Then came that dreadful phone call. Des rushed to the Townsville Hospital to find out what had happened. Gradually he was able to piece the story together. Neither Karin's parents nor her brother had been at home, and she had been attacked by four men and raped.

Worse still, the perpetrators were some of the Aborigines Des had welcomed into the church, much against the advice of some of his colleagues.

Karin's parents, who were cell leaders in Des's church, had gone around the corner to counsel a couple who were having a fight, and her brother had gone out and left the lights on. As Karin opened the front door, the men were in the house waiting for her, and she didn't stand a chance.

Now she was lying in a hospital bed, her young life ebbing away.

Des was absolutely distraught, and he prayed like

never before. He knew the power of God could turn around desperate situations like these, but sadly, this time there was not to be any divine intervention. Karin's injuries were to prove fatal, and she died in the early hours of the morning.

How do you recover from something like this? Des was choked up with grief and guilt, both strangling the life out of him at the same time. What could he possibly say to her parents, who would now never be his in-laws?

It was all too much for the nineteen-year-old minister to cope with, particularly the criticism he received from some members of his congregation. He realized he would have to hand over the church and return to New Zealand. But first he had to attend a long and upsetting court case, where all the details of the murder and rape were regurgitated time after time.

Many in Des's church had been unhappy about the number of Aborigines in the congregation, saying that it created racial tension, and now this tragic incident was the last straw. However, Karin's parents were not in the least bit racist and had opened their home to many of the Aboriginal converts, and these four men had been part of their home cell.

Formerly they had been drug addicts and alcoholics, but had been growing in the Lord as they received discipleship training. However, they had come into contact with a former leader in the church who had resigned because of Des's policy of inclusion.

An all out racist, he had told them Des was preaching a lie, that they couldn't possibly be saved, 'because they didn't possess a soul'. The men became very angry after this and started drinking again.

The more they drank, the angrier they became, and

they decided to go to their cell leaders' house and confront them. They, of course, weren't there, so the men broke into the house to vent their anger, and shortly afterwards Karin walked into this awful trap.

The four men then raped her and beat her up so badly that when her parents found her, it was too late to save her. She had so much internal bleeding that she couldn't possibly have survived. They were beside themselves with grief and, understandably, Des was blamed because he had been responsible for their daughter.

'All I could do was to take the full blame, but I was devastated,' Des recalls, 'and I was angry with myself because I hadn't listened to God, and angry with God because He had allowed this to happen. And in my heart I wanted revenge against the Aborigines – I wanted their blood.'

The four men were quickly rounded up by the police, who matched their fingerprints to those at the murder scene, and once they were arrested, each of them confessed to what they had done.

'I will never forget that court case, as these four young men cried their eyes out, pleading for forgiveness and mercy,' Des recalls, 'but at the time, I couldn't forgive them. All I wanted was for them to pay. I had showed them the love of God and they had returned it with nothing but heartache. That was my attitude, and I knew it was wrong, but I couldn't forgive them. At the time I felt that they deserved to die.'

From then on it was downhill for Des as he struggled to preach to his congregation. His heart was filled with unforgiveness, and worse still, the devil tormented him night and day. 'Your fiancée's blood is upon your hands,' he kept telling Des. 'And those young men's lives are finished because of you, and they will never find God again.'

Clearly, Satan had engineered this situation to derail Des's ministry, and even as he battled to move beyond the valley of despair, the stark reality of the tragedy kept knocking him back into guilt and depression.

'We told you those Aborigines were no good,' some of the church people told Des. 'We told you they would only cause trouble. Now will you listen?' Des was being confronted in every direction and he realized he had to move on, but he didn't know how.

'The church actually recovered quite quickly and before long it was back in a good place, as the Lord continued to move by His grace, but the truth was that I was in a bad place,' Des says. 'Some people told me to hang in there, that I would get over it, but I felt like such a hypocrite behind the pulpit, and I eventually decided to step down.'

By this time, Des had trained up a number of leaders who were capable of running the church, and he was able to hand it over to them and move back to New Zealand, where he hoped to be restored. But it would be a whole year before he was back on his feet.

A Scripture Des learnt to cling onto during this painful period was this well-known verse from Philippians:

Not that I have already attained, or am already perfected; but I press on, that I may lay hold of that for which Christ Jesus has also laid hold of me. Brethren, I do not count myself to have apprehended; but one thing I do, forgetting those things which are behind and reaching forward to those things which are ahead, I press toward the goal for the prize of the upward call of God in Christ Jesus.

Philippians 3:12–14

'I could relate very closely to the Apostle Paul and the terrible things he did to persecute the church as Saul of Tarsus, and yet God had forgiven him and he had spent the rest of his life building up the body of Christ. His example was a great encouragement to me.'

Finally, Des came to realize that even though he had messed up and disobeyed the Lord, he had a choice to stay where he was or to move on, recognizing that he was not perfect, but a sinner saved by grace, who had to renew his mind through the Word.

'It was during this time that I came to understand the meaning of God's amazing grace,' Des says. 'Just as the old hymn goes, I was a complete wretch, but through God's grace I was completely saved.

'I was also encouraged to know that the writer of that song was the captain of a slave ship who had committed many seemingly unforgivable atrocities against mankind, and yet when he received the Lord, he received the same great forgiveness that is available to everyone who will repent of their sin and follow Jesus.

'Finally, I realized that even though I had made such a huge mistake, and although somebody had died because I didn't listen to God, the Lord had forgiven me and I now had. to overcome the devil's lies and the guilt and condemnation, and press on with my divine calling.

'I had to discipline my mind, rebuke the devil and claim Scriptures like Romans 8:1 – "There is no condemnation for them which are in Christ Jesus, who walk not after the flesh, but after the Spirit." And after many months of doing this, I was able to get back into the full-time ministry, although in a different way.

'I was finally able to forgive those men who had caused

me such pain, as well as myself, and I was able to come to terms with my unforgiveness – something the Lord has used to enable me to minister more effectively in helping to bring reconciliation between people of different races and cultures in the continent of Africa.'

And so, Des became an itinerant minister and conference speaker, focusing on mass evangelism and church planting across New Zealand and other nations, and finally he was able to put this incident behind him. It was during this time that he met up with Ros once again, who was also a great pillar of strength in helping him to recover.

All the while God, in His great love and mercy, was raising up another woman, right in front of his eyes, who had a passion for missions and a heart for Africa, where Des knew he was ultimately called.

And so a new chapter opened in Des's life as he proposed to Roslynn Brown on Mount Manganui beach in New Zealand. 'Well, what are you waiting for?' she had blurted out as they were walking together along the seashore. 'Are you going to marry me or not?'

It was a bold move, but Ros is a bold woman, who is sold out to God and eager to fulfil his every command. And there is nothing like a little nudge to get a man to commit! His healing complete, Des had to laugh at this mammoth question, but his heart was filled with peace, and he knew deep within that this romance would not end in tears, and God would use it to impact the nations.

'The Lord makes all things beautiful in His time,' Ros concludes. 'He is the only one who can take our heartaches, tragedies and pain, and turn them around. For He causes all things to work together for good, for them that love Him and are called according to his purpose' (Romans 8:28).

He is the only one who can help us deal with our pasts, and release us into our futures.

Chapter 9

Dying is Easy,
Living is the Challenge

For me, to live is Christ, and to die is gain.
Philippians 1:21

Why are some Christians so afraid of dying? Especially when they know exactly where they are going when they die. The Bible tells us very clearly that to be absent from the body is to be present with the Lord. In other words, the moment we leave this earth, we go directly to heaven and straight into the Lord's presence.

The Lord showed Des many things as his body lay in Hamilton's intensive care unit, his heart monitor flatlining, and medical personnel scurrying around trying to revive him. Now we pick up the story of his heavenly experience once again.

'I feel so drained,' Des told the Lord as they walked together on a vast pathway that extended as far as he could see. There was such a bright light radiating from it that Des was becoming weaker and weaker.

But on either side of the road there were many different trees, with people picking fruit, and passers-by were stopping to help themselves to what was in the baskets, all along the way.

'Take one!' the Lord said as Des picked up what looked like a cross between a citrus fruit, an apple and a pear. As he held it in his hands, it started to glow like solid gold.

'Partake,' said the Lord. 'It will renew your strength.'

Des took a bite, thinking he was going to break his teeth, for on the outside it had a hard, golden shell. Yet inside it was soft, and immediately it gave him a new lease of life. It tasted better than anything on earth, and gave him a sense of fulfilment, and memories of the most enjoyable times he had ever experienced. All this came together in one bite, bringing total peace and fulfilment.

Now completely re-energized, Des listened to the conversation of the many different people walking to and fro on this glorious highway, giving praise to God. 'Holy, Holy, Holy is the Lord,' he could hear them say as he read their minds. 'He is worthy, He is righteous, How mighty He is.'

As they came over the horizon, all they could see was a colossal building, with massive pillars forming a grand entrance-way that seemed to go on forever. And once again, there were statues, all placed in unending rows, and many staircases leading upwards into the building.

The closer Des got towards the building, the weaker he became, but the sound coming from it was so exhilarating. 'Holy, Holy is the Lord God Almighty, who is worthy, the Lamb who is worthy' was all he could hear in thunderous unison.

They came to twelve creatures that looked like they were made from stone, but Des could see that they were alive. One had a head like an eagle and a body like a lion, while another was in the form of a huge bear, but he had wings like a bird. They all bowed low before the Lord as He passed by.

Des was overawed, but there was still much more to come. They started to climb a set of white marble stairs, which were the most beautiful Des had ever seen. The marble was inlaid with gold, which sparkled brilliantly in the light, with gold baskets on either side of each step, overflowing with fruit.

As he walked, Des realized he could not go on. The glory was so heavy, he had to keep stopping to replenish his strength, by eating another of the golden fruits. Finally they got to the top, and all they could see was a mass of people, and all they could hear was the most beautiful sound of a thousand orchestras.

There was such a presence of the Lord, and a sense of peace as glorious worship flowed from the many choirs and the sea of people. Des could hear the sounds of a violin, then a flute, followed by a triumphant drum roll.

'This was the most amazing thing to comprehend,' Des recalls. 'I can't even explain it fully.'

As they continued to walk together, people stopped to worship the Lord. 'You are worthy, Lord, you are the Lamb!' The tallest beings, with large wings, also stopped to bow down on their knees before Jesus.

'Follow Me. I still have much to show you,' the Lord said, leading Des into a cavernous room which looked like a military headquarters. Lined up for miles were regiments of soldiers for as far as the eye could see – millions of soldiers ready for battle. Then a great door opened and the soldiers seemed to be swallowed up by a tunnel, pulling them towards earth.

'Lord, what is this? What are these men doing?' asked Des.

'These are My warrior angels, who are released on the

122

command of My Father, and they go down to the earth to fight the spiritual battles that My people face.

'Many times you have said, "Lord, I don't know how I am going to overcome this", and I hear every prayer, and I intercede on your behalf, and when I plead your case before My Father, He commands these angels to be released on your behalf to fight back the demonic forces.

'This is the heavenly army that has come to your rescue many times before, when you have been up against severe spiritual opposition, when you have been praying...

'This is what you are seeing. These warriors have been assigned to My children on earth, who are praying and asking for help.'

Des was amazed to see that some of the soldiers were in the shape of men, while others were much bigger, with wings on their backs, but all of them were fearless. Failure was not even a consideration – they knew they were being sent out to conquer.

Then he looked down into the tunnel, where he could see a legion of these mighty warriors surrounding a mass of slimy beings, who were screeching at each other in torment. They were hovering over a family on earth and wreaking havoc in their home.

'These are demon spirits,' the Lord said, pointing to the slimy creatures. 'They are Jezebellic spirits who are trying to break up this family. They have been interfering behind the scenes to get an evil woman to seduce this man into adultery.

'This family belongs to Me. They are My children and have been having great trouble in their marriage. The husband has been tempted by another woman and the wife has been crying out for My help.'

One minute the evil beings resembled a beautiful

woman, and the next you could see their deceitful, filthy nature. Some of them were sitting on the husband's shoulder talking into his ear for hours on end, justifying his wayward behaviour, and impeding his ability to reason.

As the battle for this family continued, the commander of the angels of the Lord addressed the commander of the spirits of darkness and told him to take his troops and leave. Immediately the lesser demons began to tremble with fear and started to disperse, while others cowered in the darkness, trying to hide. You could see demons running in all directions – there was no unity among them.

'You stay here!' the evil commander shouted, as more and more of his troops scattered, but it was only the high-ranking demons that stayed. And so a battle ensued, with the angels of the Lord quickly overpowering the demonic forces.

The spiritual oppression over the family now lifted, and the husband began to see clearly and realize the error of what he was doing. He opened the Bible and started reading the Word and repented. Then he approached his wife and asked her for her forgiveness, and so reconciliation began to flow...

Des was amazed by the distinct parallels between the physical world and the world of the spirit, and how the struggles facing people on earth seemed to be mirrored by a battle in the heavenlies. He thought of that Scripture in Ephesians that he knew so well:

> *For we do not wrestle against flesh and blood, but against principalities, against powers, against the rulers of the darkness of this age, against spiritual hosts of wickedness in the heavenly places.*

Ephesians 6:12

This was a revelation Des had long understood – he knew the best way to solve a problem or win a battle was through prayer, not by retaliating impulsively in the natural, but by taking the situation to the Lord and getting His divine strategy on how best to proceed.

He also knew all about the spiritual opposition he and the church leaders in Tokoroa has been up against, taking on the local witch doctors. All hell had broken loose, and he was now lying lifeless in a hospital bed, about to be taken to the mortuary.

This was now a practical lesson in spiritual warfare. The Lord had given him an insight into how demonic activity could wreak havoc in people's lives and the need to pray and take authority over the situation in the name of Jesus. As this wife did this, on the earth, so God's mighty warriors were unleashed to battle against the forces of darkness in the heavenlies.

And as Ros's father, Pastor Gordon, cried out to the Lord in that intensive care unit at Hamilton Hospital, God was going to turn the whole situation around. His passionate intercession would not go unanswered.

What Satan had meant for evil, the Lord was going to turn to good. Not only would Des be raised up from his deathbed, but he had experienced heaven in a way that would inspire him for the rest of his life.

Not only would he be completely healed from a mysterious sickness that the devil and his cohorts had brought upon him, but the Lord was to give Des a vivid insight into the fires of hell that still motivates him daily to preach the Gospel to those facing a lost eternity, not out of some legalistic duty but out of love.

In fact, this out-of-the-body experience would impact Des's life so profoundly that he would never be the same again. Through it, he would come to realize that the only reason for him to live was to serve his Lord Jesus Christ, and death was not a punishment but a reward.

Even so, the Lord was to show him that there was still much to be done before he received that reward. 'It's much easier to die for Christ,' he thought to himself, 'than to live for Him!'

Indeed, living for Christ has brought many challenges into the lives of this missionary couple from New Zealand, but both Des and Ros would not have it any other way. For them it is joy to serve the Lord, and they are prepared for the battles ahead.

Des was to learn a number of lessons from the heavenly beings he met during this experience, and the Lord would personally show him much of what was still to come in his life, which has been a guiding influence ever since.

'I spoke to you in a rubbish dump and told you things that you would do,' the Lord said to Des. 'You have been faithful, and have done what I have asked of you, but now I am revealing the bigger picture to you.

'I will take you from country to country and show you where you will serve Me, so that when you come to that place, you will know that this is where you are meant to be.'

And so the Lord began to reveal to Des much of what he would experience in Africa and Asia in the face of radical Islam. 'I will show you the power of healing,' He said, 'because the only way you will convert people from another religion to Christianity is by showing them My fire and My power.

'You have to understand the power of healing and miracles, for I will save Muslims through the power of the Gospel, through signs and wonders and miracles.

'In My name you will pray for the blind and their eyes will be opened; in My name you will pray for the deaf and their ears will hear. 'In My name you will pray for people with leprosy and they will be cleansed, and those who cannot walk will rise up and run!

'This is the only way you will convert someone of another faith – by proclaiming freedom and healing through Jesus. Then call them forth so they can serve Me.'

It was these words which had sustained Des in West Africa when things had seemed so hopeless; and it was also this prophetic experience which had led him so directly to that church in Australia, and which would lead him to settle in Africa.

Another country the Lord showed Des at this time, where he would later become involved, was the Philippines. Des remembers standing with the Lord outside a little church in a poor community in Asia. It was at night and there was very little light, as the people only had a few candles, but through the darkness Des could see a number of people praying.

They were speaking a foreign language, but he could understand them perfectly. They were pleading for the Lord to reveal Himself to the people around them, asking Him to enable them to reach out on a practical level.

'Lord, open the eyes of the blind and use us to win souls for Your Kingdom,' they prayed. 'Enable us to take care of the orphans and feed the poor. Lord, help us, so that we can be Your hands and feet and reveal Your love to our neighbourhood.'

The Lord stood listening with tears in His eyes, but there was a sense of joy in what He was hearing.

'Lord, what are You going to do?' asked Des.

'I have brought you here because I want you to do

something here. You will get involved in this church and be a part of my answer to this community.'

The Lord then led Des into a large stadium, where he saw himself preaching to thousands of people in a strange language.

'You will see my abundant provision for the people of this island. I will use you to feed these people, both physically and spiritually,' the Lord said. 'You will also be involved in humanitarian work here for My glory, and you will take care of these orphans.

'Take heed of the pastor and the elders so that you know them, so that when the time comes, you will recognize them and know that it is by My leading that you are to be involved in this nation.'

Several years later, while on a trip to Manila, what the Lord had shown Des so clearly through this experience began to unfold before his eyes. Not only did he minister in that exact village church where people had been praying for revival, but he was the scheduled speaker at a crusade in the very same stadium where he had previously walked with Jesus.

The only problem was that on the day he was meant to minister, the interpreter didn't turn up on time. He lived seventy miles away in northern Manila and had been caught in traffic.

A large crowd had gathered for the meeting and the local church band were keeping the crowd busy with extended praise and worship, but the people were getting impatient and some had started to leave.

'I must start preaching at once,' Des tried to communicate to his hosts. 'Will one of you interpret for me?' But none of them felt their English was good enough.

'Lord, what am I going to do?' Des prayed.

Des and Ros Sinclair.

Having come to the Lord miraculously on a rubbish dump in New Zealand, Des and his wife Ros are never far from ministering the Gospel in places where others may not venture, like this rubbish dump in South Africa. Here the Life Evangelism International (LEI) team ministered powerfully to the local people, praying for healing and handing out gloves and blankets to help equip them for winter.

Des preaches the word of God with a passionate conviction and with 'signs following' as many are healed of all kinds of medical conditions as he prays for the sick.

Des and Ros have a heart for the nations of the world, especially the precious children of Africa.

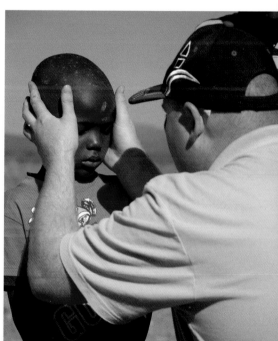

Ros ministering along with the LEI team and overseeing the distribution of food, blankets and clothing to the poor.

Des preaching at a LEI crusade. The LEI truck makes crusades like these possible and Des and Ros have plans to build an even bigger mobile trailer which can be used to accommodate trainee evangelists and double up as a platform for ministry to hold more and more crusades in outlying towns and villages in Africa.

Winning a soul to Jesus Christ is the greatest miracle of all. Each one of these precious hands represents a decision for the Kingdom and that is what LEI is all about. Each person who makes a commitment is asked to fill out a decision card to ensure effective follow up.

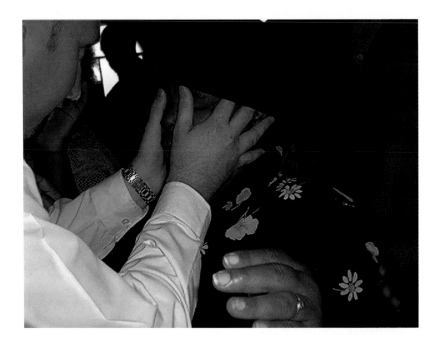

One of the many accounts of miraculous healing in Des and Ros Sinclair's ministry. This blind woman is from Miracle Valley Church in Soshenguve township in South Africa. Following the example of Jesus, Des took some mud and put it on her eyes and prayed for her to receive her sight back. As the woman cleansed her eyes, she was completely healed. 'I can see! I can see!' she shouted with great joy.

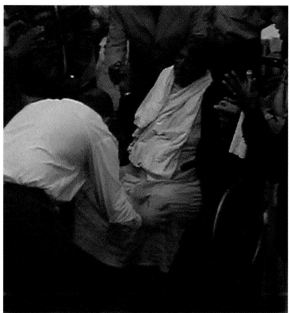

Another example is that of a lady in a wheelchair at Apostolic Faith Mission Church who got up and walked for the first time in twelve years. Her back had been broken in a car accident, but having been prayed for she got up out of her wheelchair and started to walk behind it, pushing it along for balance. Then she let her wheelchair go and started walking down the middle aisle unaided.

Des and Ros dressed in the 'royal robes' they received from one of the kings of Ghana (see chapter 7). Des met King Otumfuo, 'the Asantehene' and leader of the Ashanti people of Ghana in Kumasi on a number of occasions while he was in West Africa, where he was afforded royal protection.

Ros Sinclair stands beneath a sign marking the equator in Kenya where she and Des ministered for several months, bringing God's love into this volatile region of Africa (see chapter 11). While they were in Kenya, the town of Nyeri saw great revival and reconciliation between people of warring tribes.

'Get up and preach,' came the unexpected reply into his spirit.

'But, Lord, I don't know any Filipino, and none of the pastors will interpret...'

'Well, haven't I given you the gift of speaking in tongues?'

'Yes, Lord!'

'Well, then, get up and preach!'

Des immediately began to think about what he had read in the book of Acts – how people had heard the wonders of God declared in their own mother tongue.

'Well, Lord, you did it at Pentecost, so I guess there is no reason why people won't understand me, if I speak in tongues. Please, Lord, give me the ability to speak the local dialect!'

So Des stood up, opened his mouth and started speaking in tongues. He had no idea what he was saying, yet people started to respond, waving their hands and shouting.

This went on for some forty minutes until the interpreter finally arrived. 'Where have you been?' Des asked him the moment he came up on the stage. 'Hurry and get your microphone – we need to preach the message.'

He looked at Des, dumbfounded. 'You have already preached the message!'

'No, I haven't. We haven't even started.'

'Yes you have. I have been here for a while, and you've just preached one of the best Gospel messages in our mother tongue I have ever heard. You have just given a salvation call and you are asking people to come forward. Turn around and look – they are all coming forward now. You never told us you could speak fluent Tagalog!' (That is the most common language spoken in the Philippines.)

'I can't,' said Des, 'but God can!'

Following this amazing incident, Des was sharing with business people in Australia about the immense poverty of the islands and how the Lord wanted to bless the community there. Much to his amazement, he was given a gift of 1 million Australian dollars towards community projects, including orphanages and schools.

'God literally rebuilt that community,' Des recalls today. 'We didn't ask for the money, we didn't look for it – it just came, and the Lord fulfilled what He had shown me, exactly as He said He would.'

Looking back today, Des recalls Pastor Gordon's anguish as he lay supposedly dead in hospital, and how easily that could have been the end of his life. But God had supernaturally raised him up from his deathbed to complete a number of divine assignments.

Little did he realize then that the Lord would take him around the world to ultimately settle in South Africa, and that this prophecy concerning the conversion of many Muslims would be fulfilled exactly as the Lord had said: firstly in West Africa, where through the working of miracles, a Muslim man was raised back to life and a community was saved; then in other countries like Kenya, where the Lord was to call Des and Ros to spend several months, and where God would pour out some of the greatest miracles they have encountered in their ministry.

For Des and Ros, this is what living for Christ is all about: making every day of their lives count for the Kingdom of God.

Chapter 10

You'd Better Talk... or Die!

'Tell us what we want to know, or we will kill you!'

'Who are you spying for? Why are you here in Angola? Are you a diamond smuggler or just a spy?' The questions kept coming at Des in droves. Dehydrated, sleep-deprived and starving, he struggled to give a coherent answer... but then the intense pain would jolt him back to reality.

'Tell us what we want to know, or we will kill you!' shouted one of the interrogators as Des desperately tried to understand his garbled mix of English and Portuguese. Through his bleary eyes, he could just make out the frame of his merciless captor, holding a rubber whip made from strips of old tyres.

It was the year 2000 and Des was on his way to Luanda, the capital of Angola, for a mass crusade. He had been invited by many pastors to visit this former Portuguese colony in south-western Africa, and now the day had come.

Kissing Ros goodbye at the airport in Johannesburg, he was full of expectations about what the Lord would do through him in this troubled African nation in the coming

131

days. But, unfortunately, he would hardly get past the organizational phase of the crusade.

While a faithful band of volunteers from different churches were rigging up the stadium, Des had been invited to travel further north of Luanda to meet some pastors who wanted to get involved in the meetings, but as he was driving, he felt an urgent need to return to the crusade grounds immediately.

Even before the pick-up truck he was driving entered the stadium that had been hired for the crusade, Des could see something was wrong. A number of men were harassing the church leaders, trying to stop them from setting up for the meeting.

They did not look like the local police or authorities and were haphazardly dressed in partial military uniform, some with camouflage jackets and heavy boots and many carrying AK47 rifles.

A stranger to the volatile politics of war-ravaged Angola, Des did not realize who he was up against, whether it was MPLA or UNITA guerrillas – to him it made no difference, for he knew that Satan was the real enemy at work, trying once again to disrupt the preaching of the Gospel. Nevertheless, these men were armed and had already started to beat up one of his helpers.

'What are you doing here?' they had shouted at him. 'Why are you here with this white guy? You must be a traitor!'

Concerned for the lives of the local church members, Des immediately intervened: 'If you have a problem, you need to speak to me,' he shouted.

'Well, you'd better come with us,' came the daunting reply.

Des thought that he could reason with the men, and that since he was a foreigner from New Zealand, they would focus on him and leave the local church people alone. He thought international law was in his favour and they had no reason to detain him, so he agreed to go with the men – but he had sorely underestimated the situation.

The guerrillas grabbed Des and put him on the back of a dilapidated military vehicle. It seemed like they drove for hours, eventually stopping at their campsite, where Des was shoved into an old prison cell.

Then the beatings began. He was taken into a room where he was questioned by one man and assaulted by another. 'Tell us who you work for! Tell us why you are here!'

'I am not an Angolan – I am a New Zealander,' Des replied, 'and I am here to preach the Gospel to all men. I know nothing about your war. I am not here for war, I am here for peace. I don't take sides with any army or party or view.'

At this, the men got very upset. 'So you are here to bring peace to our enemy?' the one shouted, while the other lashed out at him. The rubber cut deep into his skin, and the wound started to bleed.

'I am here for all men,' Des answered softly.

'Then you are our enemy!' the interrogator snapped at Des, 'and we will show you what we do with our enemies.' And so the beatings continued. Many times over the next ten days the solders beat Des with wooden batons and threw stones at him.

'Lord, no weapon formed against me shall prosper,' Des cried out in his heart, yet very soon his whole body was black and blue. Unable to take much more, Des yelled out loud in agony and started to shout at the devil at the top of his voice. 'Get behind me, Satan!' he yelled. 'You have no authority over me!'

When he was finally taken back to his cell, Des was comforted by thoughts of the first Apostles, who had suffered so many things for the sake of the Gospel. 'Lord, I thank You for the privilege of being persecuted for Your sake,' he sobbed, 'but please give me the strength to survive this.'

The beatings went on for days. He was given nothing to eat and no water, and grew physically very weak. Even so, Des still tried to reason with the guards in simple English, sharing the Gospel as best he could. At times he would also pray out loud in tongues.

One time, as he was being dragged back to his cell after a beating, Des started to pray in tongues. Immediately great fear overcame his captors. Des heard one of them say, 'We did not know that this man speaks fluent Portuguese!'

Instead of throwing Des back in his cell, they put him down gently, and one of the guards had tears in his eyes. Des knew that God had touched him. 'Please, we don't want to do this,' he said in broken English, 'but we have no option – otherwise we will be killed.'

Days of interrogation and beatings had literally drained the life out of Des, and he had eaten nothing and was desperately thirsty in the Angolan heat. In fact, it seemed as though God had utterly abandoned him.

'Lord, You have to get me out of here!' Des cried out, hardly able to move due to the pain all over his body.

'My grace is sufficient for you,' said the assuring voice of God that Des had come to know so well since his days on that rubbish dump in New Zealand.

'If you tell us what we want to hear, you will make it easier for yourself,' were the last words Des heard as he blacked out. Stones had been thrown at him and one of the rebels had kicked him in the chest, breaking three of his ribs and cracking some of his vertebrae.

When Des regained consciousness, he had lost all feeling in his legs and could no longer walk. 'Lord, take my life,' he called out to God. 'This is too much! Show me Your mercy. I want to come home, Lord. Please take me home.'

God's answer was both simple and profound: 'My grace is sufficient for you. You can't come home yet, as you have not finished the work I have predestined for you. Have faith, and you will see My hand deliver you.'

Des's whole life flashed before him as he began to think about all the things he had done and how he could have served God better. Then the breakthrough came. Ten days after his abduction, United Nations peacekeeping troops burst into his cell.

At this stage Des was too dazed to realize exactly what was going on, but he remembers seeing soldiers with blue berets on their heads, who spoke to him in French.

'Why can't I feel my legs?' he asked them. Des was put on a stretcher and taken to a hospital where he was quickly put on a drip.

'We are sending you home to South Africa,' the French doctor said. 'We have no X-ray machines here, but I think you will be okay. You have a number of broken ribs and possibly some cracked vertebrae, and a lot of bruising and swelling around your spine, but I think you are going to be fine.'

After the doctor had given him an injection to relax his muscles and help with the swelling, Des was flown from Luanda to Johannesburg in a cargo plane.

At Lanseria Airport, some friends came to collect him. He was barely able to walk, but managed to get into their vehicle. Though well meaning, they had no idea of the severity of Des's condition. The rough gravel road leading to the ministry complex where they were staying added insult to injury.

Throughout this trip Ros knew nothing about her husband's abduction and torture, and even though the church in Angola had tried to get help from the authorities, nobody had contacted her.

When Des finally arrived home, he was in agony, and in no state to tell Ros anything about his time in Angola. Everything just seemed to be too much. He managed to walk the next morning and go for a short stroll around the back of the house, but suddenly collapsed in a heap on the ground, his body lying motionless, turning a worrying pale-blue colour.

Two workers on the base where Des and Ros were staying saw Des on the ground and carried him back inside the house on a stretcher.

'This is not possible! What is going on here?' Ros asked herself as anxious thoughts flew through her head. It would only be much later that she would hear all about Des's ordeal, but in the meantime she rallied to nurse her husband, without appearing too shocked.

'Let me get you into bed, my darling,' she said, but Des was in too much pain to be moved. 'Leave me on the floor,' he answered, 'and I will be all right.' Neighbours, including some paramedics who came to visit Des, also encouraged him to get up, but he remained lifeless on the floor, and though he tried, he just couldn't sit up.

'Please don't move me – I can't handle the pain,' he told Ros. 'Just get Carol to come over as soon as possible!'

By now the seriousness of the situation was beginning to dawn on Ros and she went to call their radiologist friend.

'Carol, it's Des – he has hurt himself badly and can't move. Please, we need you to come over immediately!'

'His body is going into shock,' Carol quickly diagnosed. 'We need to get him to hospital at once. He seems to have a great deal of pain in his ribs, but no feeling in his legs. This means there is something very wrong with his back.'

Once again Des had to face the excruciating pain of travelling along the dirt road in the back of a pick-up truck, and it seemed like it took forever to reach Olivedale Clinic.

The doctors who examined Des were astounded when they saw the extent of his condition. X-rays revealed that he had sustained major damage to his spinal cord. Three of his vertebrae had split, and he would need extensive surgery to pin them back together. 'We don't believe you will ever walk again,' was the awful diagnosis.

Ros now had to come to terms with the situation, and the possibility that her husband would be in a wheelchair for the rest of his life, but she remained strong in faith. 'Lord, I just hand this situation over to you,' she prayed. 'Whether Des ever walks again or is in a wheelchair for the rest of his life, we will carry on preaching the Gospel. We are not going back to New Zealand. You have called us here and we will carry on regardless.'

She had been there when Des had received the prophecies over his life as a young boy, and knew that God still had much to accomplish through them as a couple. She had felt the call to Africa herself, and this had been confirmed to her many times.

'I refuse to receive this report,' was her ongoing confession. 'I don't receive this. It is not right. God has called us to Africa. I know what the prophecies say, and half of them have not come to pass yet. I know we are going to carry on, therefore I don't receive this wheelchair.'

Meanwhile a great deal was going through Des's mind as he continued proclaiming healing Scriptures and trusting the Lord for his healing. 'Devil, you have no authority over me,' he declared. 'I don't believe I am going to be disabled for the rest of my life. I can't complete the mission God has called me to in a wheelchair.'

No matter how much Des claimed his healing, it did not look like there was any change in the situation. Many great men of God came to pray for and encourage Des while he was in hospital, including some international evangelists, and Dr Marvin Wolford, a missionary who had spent many years in Central Africa.

'You know what your problem is?' Dr Wolford shared with Des. 'You have a list as long as your arm about why God should heal you, and you have another list of what you have done for God. You need to realize that all you have achieved for God belongs to Him. Have you even taken the time to thank the Lord for saving your life? If you will touch the Lord, then God will touch you.'

And so Des began to thank the Lord from the bottom of his heart, and as he prayed with this veteran missionary to the Congo, he felt the warmth of the Holy Spirit upon his body. That night the Lord ministered to Des from Mark 5 – the story of the woman with the issue of blood:

Now a certain woman had a flow of blood for twelve years, and had suffered many things from many physicians. She had spent all that she had and was no better, but rather grew worse. When she heard about Jesus, she came behind Him in the crowd and touched His garment. For she said, 'If only I may touch His clothes, I shall be made well.' Immediately the fountain of her blood was dried up, and she felt in her body that she was healed of the affliction. And Jesus, immediately knowing in Himself that power had gone out of Him, turned around in the crowd and said, 'Who touched My clothes?'

Mark 5:25–30

God clearly showed Des that those who came to worship Jesus, those who came to touch Him, had received healing. He was saying to Des, 'I cannot touch you, my son, because you are acting like one of the crowd. Reach out now and touch Me, and I will touch you!'

Des realized that his thoughts were preoccupied with himself and his condition, and he had stopped worshipping the Lord. 'Lord, forgive me,' he cried. 'I will continue to serve You, no matter what. I will do the best I can for You, even if I am in a wheelchair. Thank You for Your redeeming grace.'

And so Des went to sleep with a song of worship in his heart, and when he awoke the next morning, he could feel his feet again for the first time in two weeks, and the pain in his ribs had disappeared. He looked over at the patient next to him and asked, 'Are my feet moving?'

'It looks like it!' was all the confirmation Des needed.

'If I can feel my legs, I should be able to sit up,' Des thought to himself, as he sat up straight in the bed. 'And if I can sit up and I can feel my legs again, then I should be able to walk!'

He threw his legs over the edge of the bed and sat there for a few moments, while the man in the bed next to him frantically tried to get the nurse's attention by ringing his buzzer.

'You can't do that!' he yelled at Des hysterically. 'You have to stay perfectly still in your condition.'

As the nurse entered the room, she took one look at Des and started shouting at him, *'Stay where you are, Mr Sinclair! Don't move. You can't walk!'*

'Wanna bet?' Des shouted back at her. 'All things are possible with my God!'

He then proceeded to stand up and walk straight towards her.

At that very moment, a colleague of Des named Corné came into the room to visit him, and he saw a miracle unfold. This so-called paralysed man was no longer lying motionless in his bed. He was now walking though the corridors of the hospital, shouting at the top of his voice: 'The Lord has healed me! Come and see a man who has touched Jesus!'

Pretty soon, Des had a crowd of fellow patients around him and doctors and nurses staring in utter amazement. Never one to miss an opportunity, he began to share the Gospel with renewed strength as he testified to the healing power of Jesus Christ.

What Satan had meant for evil, God had turned into good. Once again the Sinclairs had received an amazing miracle from God. It would thrust them into the next season of their ministry in Africa.

And what of Angola? 'In God's timing, I will go back there and finish the crusade I started!' Des maintains.

Chapter 11

Back to the Rubbish Dump

KENYA

You shall build the old waste places.
Isaiah 58:12

Shortly after Des and Ros moved to South Africa from New Zealand in 1998, the Lord led them to East Africa for a period of five months.

'I want you to go to Nyeri, Kenya,' He told Des. 'I want you to plan a crusade and bring revival for Me in that place. It is My time and I want you to go in person and take your wife with you, and live amongst the people, and I will use you to show My glory. I have prepared the way before you, and you will see a mighty harvest.'

Arriving in Nyeri, a town about 100 miles north of the Kenyan capital, Nairobi, the Sinclairs had a great sense of excitement that God was going to shake the city, and were full of faith that there would be great transformation, but the more the couple talked to the pastors and church leaders, the more negative was the response.

Gradually Des and Ros began to realize how ethnically diverse Kenya was as a nation, and how much tension there was between the different tribes, especially since the tribal clashes of the early 1990s, which had seen thousands of people killed and left tens of thousands homeless.

Much of this violence stemmed back to the Mau Mau war of the 1950s, when a militant African nationalist movement was formed among the Kikuyu people of Kenya, with a vow to free the country from British colonialism at any cost.

The people of the movement became known as the Mau Maus and were well known for their hostility towards other tribesmen who refused to rise up against the British, and many people were brutally murdered.

Now, after years of division in Nyeri, it was clear that there were still great rifts between people of different tribes. Whether they were from the Kikuyu tribe and supporters of the Mau Mau, or from one of the many other Kenyan tribes, they could not forgive each other or forget how brother had slaughtered brother.

There was still great bitterness amongst the different tribes, and they would not associate with each other, and nowhere was this more obvious than amongst the local churches, where pastors were quick to tell the Sinclairs about their political and ethnic differences. Des recalls that their first meeting to plan a crusade ended up in an all-out fist-fight between pastors of different denominations and cultural backgrounds, and he literally had to pull them apart from each other.

'You are brothers!' Des shouted at the six men. 'You are men of God! You cannot act like this!'

'We are not brothers,' one of the pastors shouted back, and the meeting quickly dispersed.

Des sat on one of the pews of the old Pentecostal church with his head in his hands, thinking he had made a mistake in coming to Kenya. 'Lord, I have missed it. There is no way that anything can happen here, if this is the attitude of the pastors. There is no way You can bring revival in this place.'

'No, you didn't hear Me wrong, You heard Me right,' came the Spirit's witness as Des prayed. 'This is exactly what I wanted to show you. Now, what are you going to do about it?'

'Lord, I can't do anything. You are the only One who can change the hearts of men.'

'Yes, but I have given you strategy, and you have seen transformation before. Now think of what you have done in the past, and apply it.'

Once again the Lord had spoken to Des in a profound way in an ongoing conversation with God. This doesn't happen to him all the time, but when it does, Des is always overjoyed.

So Des thought back to what they had done before in areas where there had been relational problems between different ministries, and he remembered how effective twenty-four-hour prayer and worship had been to bring churches together.

Gradually, to Des's amazement, he managed to secure the participation of a number of churches, and the local town hall provided an ideal neutral venue, where different church choirs and bands could lead praise and worship around the clock.

All of a sudden, a spiritual breakthrough started to take place. 'Now I want you to preach the Gospel on the streets,' the Lord instructed Des. 'Show them that I live, that I have risen, because they don't know Me and cannot see Me.'

So Des began to preach on street corners and in the marketplace. As people began to gather and the Holy Spirit started to move amongst them, there were many miracles of healing.

'It was just like in the New Testament,' says Ros, 'where the apostles walked past sick people and they were made whole. People were being healed without even being prayed for. It was amazing!'

News of this sovereign move of God got around very quickly, and it wasn't long before the pastors came to see what was going on. Some of them started to follow Des around and watch him as he prayed for the sick, and their hearts began to soften as they saw God open blind eyes in front of them and deaf ears were able to hear.

One by one, they asked Des to minister in their churches, and God continued to move in supernatural ways. Pastors were weeping and repenting, and within a period of a couple of months Des was able to host another meeting of the city's spiritual leaders.

This time sixty-four pastors came and there was an air of cooperation among them. They all acknowledged that God was at work within their community and wanted to be involved in a city-wide crusade.

'This was the beginning of the breakthrough,' Des recalls, yet when it came to choosing a crusade committee, he once again had to intervene, as the pastors only wanted to choose members of their own tribes.

'I am going to have to pick you, as the Spirit leads,' Des told them, choosing members of different tribes, and appointing them to meet to plan the crusade. This was clearly God at work, as this was the first time in Nyeri that pastors of different tribes had worked together.

As the crusade drew near, the Lord gave Des a vision of how He had already prepared the way through divine visitation, and Des saw angels appearing to people in the surrounding villages and how their hearts would be open to receive the Gospel.

The local pastors were not convinced. They couldn't believe that villagers from the different tribes would join together for the crusade. 'It will have to be God,' they said, and they wouldn't visit any of the neighbouring towns with Des to invite members of other tribes to attend. 'It would put our lives and your lives in great danger,' they said.

But God had given Des a very clear vision of angels appearing to tribal leaders, and telling them that a white man would come, and lead them into the presence of Almighty God, and that they should not be afraid of going into another tribe's territory, because the Lord would protect them.

That same night, the chairman of the Nyeri crusade committee had a very similar dream. He approached Des the next day and shared what he had dreamt and agreed with him that they needed to go to the other tribal groups and invite them, for the Lord had prepared the way.

Des recalls that as they entered the different villages, there was a sense that God was present! They were received with open arms, and in one village they were invited to sit and have a meal with the chief and his elders.

The chief began to share through his interpreter that a very tall man had appeared to him and his tribal leaders. 'He was dressed in white, and was as bright as the sun, and he told each of us that a white man would come in a white vehicle, and bring one of our tribal enemies with him, and we should go with them into another tribe's territory, to be brought into the true light.'

God in His mercy and compassion had reached out to bring reconciliation to an entire community through Des's obedience, and each tribal leader came to attend a combined meeting, where the Lord touched them mightily.

One leader, who was blind from injuries sustained to

his eyes during tribal clashes, had his sight fully restored, and a chief who was deaf in one ear and unable to walk was completely healed.

Because of these remarkable miracles, the tribal leaders allowed the village people to attend the crusade, and in the end more people came to the crusade from the surrounding areas than from the city of Nyeri itself.

In one of the meetings, all the pastors involved in the crusade stood before the interdenominational, intertribal congregation and joined hands together across the stage and asked for the people's forgiveness for their wrongdoings and bad attitudes.

Then they began to approach each other, asking for forgiveness and reconciling with each other. They then proceeded to hug one another and cry with remorse because of their wrong attitude towards their bothers in Christ. Never before had the people seen the pastors stand together in such unity and humility before the Lord, and there was much rejoicing and weeping, even from the crowd.

During this time of God's visitation, many were healed. In one meeting, six people who were blind in one eye and short-sighted in the other were prayed for, and all of them were able to see perfectly.

A woman who was bent over with a deformed back and had to walk with a stick, cried tears of joy as she stood upright and walked without any support. One leg had been longer than the other, but now both legs were the same length and she no longer needed her stick.

Then there was a four-year-old boy with a cancerous tumour on the side of his head. His mother told Des and the pastors that he had received the best medical care possible in Nairobi, but that nothing could be done and he was being left to die.

When Des and Ros prayed for him, he could hardly see, as he was going blind because of the effects of the tumour on his brain. But after prayer, he could see clearly, and could follow Des's hand as he moved it around. Also the lump on his head had shrunk tremendously.

In an all-night prayer meeting, as Des was preaching, a bright blue mist suddenly appeared at about one o'clock in the morning and a strong breeze blew through the congregation, knocking some of the people out of their chairs.

Then excitement broke out at the back of the church as those who had previously been disabled started to run around the building. The pastors brought a thirty-seven-year-old deaf and dumb man to Des. He had been born without eardrums and couldn't speak, but as Des prayed for him, he could immediately hear in his right ear, and after further prayer, was able to hear completely.

The pastors in the meeting then spent half an hour with the man, testing his hearing and teaching him to pronounce a few words. Since then he has learnt the local language, has given his heart to the Lord and has joined a local Assembly of God church.

This was certainly a time of divine visitation, and Ros and Des had never seen the Lord pour out His Spirit so corporately and in such great measure in one place.

Here they were, in the heart of Africa, in one of the most beautiful countries on earth, well known for its abundant wildlife and game, and near the beautiful Mount Kenya, but they were also surrounded by poverty and desperate medical conditions.

This was a place very different to their homeland of New Zealand, and Ros was upset to see the number of people begging in the streets, including many street children and frail old women carrying heavy loads on their heads and backs.

There were also slum areas that were so much worse than anything she had ever seen, but she was encouraged by all that the Lord was doing to change desperate situations. And perhaps the greatest thing that happened to her and Des during this time in Kenya was a visit to the Nyeri rubbish dump.

An Indian Kenyan pastor, Zuli Osman Allu, had been watching Ros and Des and following them around, but each time Des motioned for him to come over and talk, he seemed to hide away.

When Des asked the local pastors about this, they said, 'He is not a pastor. We don't recognize him. He is down there with the people who are going to hell.'

'What do you mean?' Des asked.

'The prostitutes, the drug addicts, the criminals – they all live in the valley on a dump, and God's judgment is upon them. He ministers to them, and we don't want anything to do with him, and you shouldn't either.'

But the Lord had already revealed to Des that here was a man who had a heart after God. He was taking care of the lost sheep, and the Lord greatly appreciated his efforts as a pastor.

'You're a pastor,' Des declared to Zuli, walking up towards him. 'You're looking after the people who are closest to the heart of the Lord! Where is this place?'

'Down in the valley,' Zuli replied softly.

'How many people are you talking about?'

'Maybe 20,000, but most of them are dying from full-blown HIV/AIDS and other STDs.'

'And you are the only pastor doing anything about it?'

'Yes, and the other pastors hate me for it. I am also an outcast.'

At this stage, some of the local pastors interrupted to take Des aside. 'You cannot be seen talking to this man,' said one of them.

'You can't associate with this man if you want us to work with you,' said another.

The Spirit of the Lord rose up within Des. 'It is not the healthy who need a doctor, but the sick,' he replied. 'Go and learn what this means!' (See Mark 2:17.)

Immediately he left the other pastors and walked away with Pastor Zuli. 'Take me to this place,' Des asked. 'I want to see where these people are.'

And so he and Ros followed the pastor down a steep hill, into the valley below. The smell of sewage, rotting flesh and death was overwhelming as they walked through crowds of poor and diseased people.

Ros and Des could not believe what they were seeing. There were people in front of them whose flesh seemed to be falling off them. It looked like they were being eaten alive. They had seen the ravages of leprosy before, but they had never seen anything like this.

'When are you having your next service?' Des asked.

'On Sunday!' Zuli answered.

'I want to come and minister with you,' Des offered.

It was a Sunday they would never forget.

As the Word was preached to the crowd assembled in the little wooden church, people continued to come in droves to hear the Gospel, and many of those present gave their hearts to Jesus.

Then, after Des had preached, he and Ros prayed for people from morning to night, and as they laid hands on people, they saw the Lord do amazing miracles in their lives.

LIFE ON THE LINE

There were six adults and children who could not hear or speak, and the Lord healed them all. Many of them had never heard any sound before. As they heard people talking for the first time, tears filled their eyes, and they began to try to communicate.

There were two women with hip deformities, who had one leg shorter than the other. God healed them by lengthening their short legs and fixing their hips. They got up and began to walk freely around the church, without pain, and threw down their crutches as they walked free from their infirmity.

Many people with HIV/AIDS were also prayed for. Some of them were so weak that they could not hold down any food or even sit up, and they had to be brought into the church on stretchers. They were right at death's door, yet later reports from the pastor confirmed that after they had been prayed for, many of them gained weight and were no longer suffering from their illnesses.

There was such a never-ending stream of people coming for prayer that some of the men living on the dump opened up a hole in the corrugated-iron roof, and using ropes, started to lower people down on stretchers, so that Des could pray for the motionless bodies lying upon them.

Des realized that the men had great faith to do this, and he started commanding disabled people to get up and walk in the name of Jesus.

All of sudden one of the men got up out of his stretcher and started walking. It was an amazing sight, and Ros and Des were very excited. It was just like a piece of the New Testament coming alive before their very eyes!

Now it happened on a certain day, as He was teaching, that there were Pharisees and teachers of

150

*the law sitting by, who had come out of every town
of Galilee, Judea, and Jerusalem. And the power of
the Lord was present to heal them. Then behold,
men brought on a bed a man who was paralyzed,
whom they sought to bring in and lay before Him.
And when they could not find how they might bring
him in, because of the crowd, they went up on the
housetop and let him down with his bed through
the tiling into the midst before Jesus. When He
saw their faith, He said to him, 'Man, your sins
are forgiven you'.*

Luke 5:17–20

Pretty soon, there were stretchers everywhere, and a constant flow of people, as those who had been healed started bringing their friends and families. But they also started bringing in bags of coffee-beans, rice, cloth and even live chickens.

When it got dark Des realized they finally had to stop. 'We can come back another time!' he told Pastor Zuli.

'These gifts are for you,' Zuli replied. 'The people want to bless you and honour you.'

Not only had they brought all kinds of provisions – they had also taken up an offering of 50,000 Kenyan shillings (about 1,000 US dollars).

'These were people who lived in cardboard boxes,' Ros recalls, 'and here they were, bringing the best they had, which was a most humbling experience.'

Des remembered the nights he had spent in his youth, huddled up in a cardboard box, but that was luxury in comparison to where these people were living. And yet he knew he had to accept their offering, or he would offend them. He also knew that refusing their gifts would deprive them of the blessing of God, since the Lord would bless them back in abundance for their giving.

'Thank you so much,' he said, smiling at the crowd of people before him, while his heart was crying out to God, 'Lord, I can't take from these people!'

Then the Lord showed Des what to do with the offering. He had prayed for a couple who had full-blown AIDS and were covered in lesions. They seemed to be much better now, and Des felt led to give them the money.

'Their only request to Me is for a wedding,' the Lord revealed to Des. 'They haven't asked for healing, but in their hearts they keep asking Me if they can be married in church before they die. I want you to give some of the offering to the pastor for their marriage ceremony and for a community celebration which everyone can attend.'

'That is exactly the only thing they have asked for,' Pastor Zuli said, receiving the money, his eyes wet with tears. And so Des and Ros distributed the offering to different people, as the Spirit led.

Pastor Zuli's testimony of what he witnessed in Nyeri appears in the Appendix to this book.

Walking along the muddy track back to their pick-up truck, Des and Ros felt that this had been the most amazing experience they had ever shared as a couple. Their actions that day would also have a positive outcome on many of the churches in the area, who in the past had not wanted to have anything to do with ministering to 'social outcasts', but the Spirit of God used Des and Ros to convict them and bring about a change of heart.

As they got into the pick-up, the couple bowed their heads before the Lord to thank Him for His love and mercy to these people, and to give Him all the glory for the miracles they had experienced that day.

Then the Lord began to whisper softly to Des, 'That's right. I brought you here for a reason, because I want you to see what I am going to do through you in South Africa.

'All eyes have been focused on South Africa because of the injustices of apartheid. But I want the world to see Me at work in that nation, and I will show My glory to the world by healing those who are dying, and many, many will testify.

'The world and Africa are looking for the answer to HIV/AIDS, but I hold the answer because I am the Creator and the Healer. Where blood tests are positive, I will cause them to come back negative. Where people's flesh seems to be falling off, I will cause new skin to grow and many people will be totally healed, with medical proof to back up their testimonies.

'I want you to finish off what you are doing in West Africa and prepare yourselves, because I now want you to focus on South Africa and the surrounding countries. I see how many people have HIV/AIDS in South Africa, and yet the Church is doing very little. That is why I have brought this to your attention.

'Also, crime is on the increase. Many South Africans are slaves of the devil, but when they look to Me, they will be released from this bondage and there will be a return to morality. My hand is upon South Africa and I will use you there and be with you.'

God had taken Des back to the dump; now He was going to use him to be a healing balm to many others living as outcasts in South Africa and to train up evangelists who, like Pastor Zuli, would reach out to those nobody wanted – those closest to God's heart.

Chapter 12

There is a Better Way

SOUTH AFRICA

The restorers of streets to dwell in.
Isaiah 58:12

'Standing in front of me was a crowd of extremely dangerous men. Some of them were convicted murderers and rapists, while others were serving sentences for all kinds of grievous crimes. And yet, instead of being scared to death, I felt God's love for them welling up in me...'

Ros Sinclair recalls her initial apprehension at venturing into a maximum-security prison for the first time in her life. 'There I was, a young Kiwi girl from the other side of the world, who had never been inside a prison before, never mind a maximum-security facility, so it was quite a scary experience. I was entirely out of my comfort zone!

'But the Lord instructs us in His Word to reach out to all who are held captive, whether they are physically behind bars or in a spiritual jail. How else will people ever know the love of God and the freedom that is available to them in Christ, unless we go and share it with them?' Ros asks.

Through the ministry of people like Des and Ros Sinclair, there are many inmates in prisons throughout the world who have come to receive the Lord Jesus Christ as their Saviour. Though they may still be serving their time, God has set them free on the inside, and today they are building the Church behind bars.

'We need to pray for our brothers and sisters in prison,' says Ros, 'for they are part of the family of God. We are all sinners saved by grace. We have all done things wrong, whatever the case may be, but the Lord still loves us equally, and if we have confessed our sin, we have been forgiven and stand righteous together in God's eyes.'

For Des Sinclair, the word 'prison' brings back harsh memories of some of the most difficult times in his life, when he was held captive and tortured in Angola and when he was imprisoned in Mali and sentenced to death. He has experienced first-hand what it is like to be behind bars, and today he can minister with great compassion and understanding to inmates.

'Jesus puts things into perspective,' says Des, 'by revealing to us that if a man looks at a woman with lust in his heart, he has already committed adultery with her. In the same way, if a person plans to do evil, they have already done so in the sight of God.

'Those who are in prison may have committed physical acts of crime or violence, but there are even more people outside of prison who are just as guilty as they are. So we are not called to judge the inmates we minister to, but to reach out to them.

'We are all guilty of sin and need a saviour. Before I met Jesus I was a prisoner. I was bound not behind physical bars, but behind spiritual bars – but Jesus revealed Himself to me and broke open those prison doors and set me free. And I now have a passion to preach a message of freedom to everyone, whether they are prisoners behind bars or people on the street who don't know Jesus.

'Both have something in common, both have an area of their lives where they are in chains, whether they are prisoners of fear, condemnation, a violent temper, addiction or anything else that keeps them in bondage.

'And only the Gospel of Jesus Christ can bring release to prisoners and set the captives free, which is why our ministry in the prisons is so important to us, because all people are behind bars to some degree, and all those who are bound need to hear the good news that Jesus is able to bring freedom into their lives.

'It is the most amazing thing to see prisoners cry and repent before the Lord and then to witness their transformation from people who are bound by guilt, remorse and anger, to living lives of peace and freedom. That is extraordinary.'

As crime continues to ravage the continent of Africa, and particularly South Africa – where the statistics for armed robbery, rape and murder continue to escalate and car hijackings and house breakings are everyday occurrences – Des and Ros believe God has raised them up to show the people of Africa that there is a better way.

They are convinced that the answer to crime lies in softening criminal hearts with the love of God and leading people of all races in repentance and reconciliation through mass evangelism. Des also believes that the Church of Jesus Christ can be instrumental in addressing crime by reaching out to and caring for disadvantaged communities and showing God's love in action.

As more and more young evangelists are raised up in a nation, the more the Gospel will impact that nation, not only in bringing crime under control, but also in addressing the HIV/AIDS pandemic and the outbreak of sexually transmitted diseases.

'It is the members of the body of Christ who are the "restorers of streets to dwell in",' says Des. 'Many of the world's streets are uninhabitable or "no-go areas" because of gang violence, racism and crime, but the Lord has called us to be "repairers of the breach".

'I am so encouraged by the increasing number of believers today who have this revelation, and it is fantastic to see so many churches in this hour who have a heart to reach out as peacemakers in situations where war and violence are rife and to take a message of hope to those in prison.

'And as we trust God together for His protection and believe Him to bring about repentance and reconciliation in our nations, we will be amazed at what the Lord will do to turn things around.'

Ros and Des have experienced the Lord's supernatural protection many times, and have seen how the Lord can intervene to change people's hearts and bring about reconciliation between different races, but little did they expect what God would do to show them some light at the end of the tunnel when it came to combating crime in their own lives.

On 8 May 2002 Des was driving to Soshenguve Township north of Pretoria, South Africa, where he was scheduled to preach at a high school. It was half past six in the morning when he was held up by four armed men.

'Get out of the car or we'll kill you!' one man said, leaning through the open window and pushing a revolver into Des's neck.

'Give me your wallet,' instructed another man.

Des was shocked. He had heard of many South Africans who had been hijacked, but he had never expected it to happen to him.

As he sat in the driver's seat, one of the hijackers grabbed his car keys, another took his wallet, and the two others pointed guns at him the whole time.

Once they had pulled Des out of the car, they dragged him behind some bushes on the side of the road and, even though they now had what they wanted, they still threatened to kill him. 'White man, you deserve to die! Prepare to meet your maker!' one of the hijackers shouted.

Des responded confidently, 'If a man is going to die, then at least let him say a few last words. Do you realize that if you murder me, you will be bringing a curse upon yourselves? My blood will be on your hands!

'God made a promise to me, just as He did with Abraham, that those who bless me will be blessed, and those who curse me will be cursed. You will pay dearly for your actions.'

A look of fear began to fall on the men's faces, boosting Des's confidence, even though he continued to stand in the line of fire. 'Do you know that you are condemned to hell unless you repent and receive Jesus?' he shouted at the hijackers. 'I rebuke you in the name of the Lord Jesus Christ!'

All of a sudden the four men took fright and ran off, as if they had seen a ghost – dropping the car keys in their haste, but stealing all the money Des and Ros had.

Des quickly picked up the keys that had fallen, got back into the car and drove away. He looked around to see what had caused the men to run – whether there was a police vehicle or a traffic officer in sight – but there was nothing. So he continued on his way to the school where he was scheduled to minister.

After sharing about the attempted hijacking to the students, and how the Lord had supernaturally protected him, Des had a tremendous response from the teenagers, with about 1,500 decisions to receive Jesus Christ as Saviour.

Both the principal and the school counsellor were delighted. This was a school where on average, three students a week were being buried from HIV/AIDS-related deaths, and they were convinced that it was only the Gospel that could make a difference.

HIV/AIDS is the number one killer in South Africa for youths between the ages of thirteen and twenty-four, and the hijacking statistics are, of course, staggering. Des had taken on two of the country's main killers in one day!

On his way home, Des thanked the Lord for His divine protection over Ros and himself, and continued to wonder what it was that had caused the hijackers to make off so quickly.

It was not until two years later, when ministering at Johannesburg Correctional Services, a maximum-security prison, that he would find out. Des was praying for inmates at the end of a service when two men came up to him. 'Do you remember us?' one of the men asked.

'Have we met before?' Des answered.

'We are the ones who tried to hijack you in Pretoria in 2002,' the other man replied.

'We nearly killed you,' the first man interrupted, obviously wanting to come clean.

The two inmates then told Des exactly what had happened during the attempted hijacking.

'So what stopped you from killing me?' Des asked. 'Why did you suddenly drop the keys to my car and run away as quickly as you could?'

'We saw a man in front of you – the tallest man we have ever seen! He was white and shone like the sun!' one inmate explained.

'We were so scared as we saw the power of your God, that we dropped everything and ran for our lives,' the other man interrupted.

'What happened to the other two?' Des asked.

'They are dead,' came the answer. Then the two men told Des how the curses he had warned them against had happened just like he had said. Their two friends had been killed in a shoot-out with the police, and they themselves had been taken into custody and sentenced for various crimes and were now serving time.

Des was amazed by this startling confession. The last thing he had ever expected was to come face to face with these men again, but the best news of all was that they had been coming to his prison outreach meetings and had given their lives to the Lord under his ministry.

'We are serving God now, and we ask you to please forgive us for what we did to you,' one of the men said.

'We are so sorry for threatening you with a gun and stealing your money,' said the other.

This is just one remarkable example of how the Lord has used Des and Ros to transform the lives of inmates in South Africa's prisons. There have been more than 2,000 recorded salvation decisions to date, for which the Sinclairs give God all the glory.

What a wonderful testimony this is! The Lord completely turned this situation around: hardened criminals, who would have thought nothing of putting a bullet through Des's head, had been touched by God, and were now serving the Lord. It could only have happened because Des made a conscious decision at the time to forgive these men and pray for their salvation.

Des had learnt a valuable lesson in Australia, through his fiancée's tragic death. It had taken some time for him to overcome the hatred he had felt towards her murderers, but by God's grace he had been able to forgive them and move on with his life.

'Had I kept all that bitterness locked up inside of me, it would have crippled me and my ministry would have been over,' Des says. 'Unforgiveness keeps people locked in the past and unable to go forward into their future.'

After all Des has been through, it has become much easier for him to forgive those who have caused him pain over the years, and to minister to those crippled with unforgiveness and racism.

Following the tragedy in Northern Queensland, Des realized he could not outlaw an entire group of people because of the actions of a minority, as that would also keep him trapped in bitterness and hatred. Ever since, he has been able to help many others overcome their racist attitudes.

'I forgave you long ago!' Des told the two prisoners, sensing a release between them. 'And I pray God's blessing over you and your families,' he said.

'The amazing thing about the Gospel is that freedom is available to all men, but it comes from within,' he told the men. 'You are cleansed by the blood of Jesus and forgiven by the grace of God, which is available to everyone who calls upon His name.'

The two men looked at Des, their faces glowing. 'That is exactly how we feel,' one of them answered. 'Now that we have received Jesus, we are free men. We are no longer bound by the terrible things that used to torment us!'

The other man was also keen to let Des know how much God had changed his life through Des's ministry. 'We may be behind bars, but we are no longer prisoners,' he said. 'When we were on the outside, we were free men, yet we were so bound. But now, even though we are still inside, because we have met Jesus, we are free!'

'How wonderful!' Des commented. 'That is such an encouragement to us who are involved in prison ministry.'

The Sinclairs have also been most encouraged by the extraordinary number of inmates who have given their hearts to the Lord, many of whom are now leading church meetings and reaching out to other prisoners. Some have even been ordained as pastors.

'It has been amazing to see the transformation of murderers, rapists and possessed men, whom psychologists have dismissed as having no chance of rehabilitation,' says Des. 'The touch of Jesus has restored their minds, and some of them are now leading the Church behind bars.

'But none of this is possible, without us overcoming the battle of condemnation and unforgiveness in our hearts. The devil loves to accuse and condemn us, but I have learnt that if we can't forgive ourselves, then we can't be forgiven by God or forgive others.

'Time is a healer,' says Des, 'but we also have to walk in forgiveness to those who have wronged us. People need to be held accountable for their actions, but no matter what they have done, God forgives them if they truly repent of their sin. And if they are forgiven by God, then what right do we have not to forgive them?

'People often feel that they are justified in holding grudges against others in their hearts, but the fact is, if they don't release these people, they will end up destroying themselves.'

Ros and Des believe that forgiveness is something that every believer today needs to keep close to their hearts, as there will always be those who offend us.

'We as believers need to realize that when people come against us, they are coming against God, and we should not take the attack personally, but rather forgive them and turn the other cheek,' Des advises. 'For, as we respond in love, the grace of God will not only increase in our lives, but this action will open the door for the Holy Spirit to minister in the lives of those who have wronged us.'

Perhaps the greatest example of reconciliation at work in the ministry of Life Evangelism International is Des and Ros's work in combating racism in South Africa. Just like Pastor Zuli in Kenya, Des has been called all kinds of derogatory names because of his love of all people and his passion to reach all cultures, and he has been told that if he continues to preach to some people groups, he will end up having no credibility in ministry.

'This has been hurtful, especially when it comes from so-called brothers in Christ. But at the end of the day I ask myself the question, "Where would Jesus be?" I'm sure He would be among the poor people of the squatter camps, among the sick and ministering to the drug-lords. That is where He would go first, as it is not the healthy who need a doctor, but the sick. I want to go where Jesus would go and be His hands and feet.'

Despite the end of apartheid, relationships between different races in South Africa are often still strained, but the Sinclairs have had remarkable success in turning this around. Des was surprised when he received an invitation to preach at the leadership conference of a church closely aligned with white supremacist teaching, but the Lord clearly told him to go.

When the time came for Des to address the all-white gathering, the large crowd was obviously put off by the fact that he spoke English and not Afrikaans, but it was about to get much worse for them! The Lord had laid a powerful message on Des's heart about the purpose of Pentecost and the fruit it brought to the New Testament Church.

'When Peter ministered on the Day of Pentecost, 3,000 people came into the Church that day – men and women of many different races and cultures, including many Samaritans, who were considered the least of all people,' Des told the church leaders in front of him. 'Pentecost shows us that all men are equal, as everyone heard the wonders of God being declared to them in their mother tongue!'

This was not what this crowd wanted to hear, and some of the people stood up and started yelling at Des. But he is not one to compromise the Scriptures, and he continued regardless:

'I am not ashamed of the Gospel, for it is the power of God for the salvation of *all* men,' he said. 'That is the truth, and I don't care if you agree with what I am saying or not. The truth will prevail.

'Racism is a state of the heart and it is sin. Nowhere in Scripture is it justified. If we say we hate our brother but yet we say we love the Lord, then the love of the Lord is not within us and we are deceived. And there is racism in the hearts of many of you, and you need to repent. Your racism will take you to hell!'

By now a large group of people had come to the front to protest against what Des was preaching. 'How dare you come in here and talk to us like this!' one of the pastors shouted. 'We don't want to hear any more.'

'Stay where you are and listen!' Des replied. 'God knows your hearts and he is giving you an opportunity to repent from your sin. Otherwise He will expose you right here and now.

'You sir,' Des said, pointing to a man on the side of the auditorium. 'You are filled with pride and your heart is filled with racism. Repent now and bow down on your knees so that God can restore you.'

The man looked at Des arrogantly. Then he spoke: 'Who are you, Englishman, to tell me what to do?'

'I am cautioning you – if you don't repent, God will reveal your sins,' Des replied, for the Lord had shown him that this was the only way the crowd would listen. 'Choose now who you will serve,' Des challenged the man, but he remained as defiant as ever.

Then Des started to operate in the word of knowledge, which immediately got the crowd's attention, silencing his hecklers. He had never seen the man before but started to tell him which city he was from and relay details that he couldn't possibly have known.

'You are a pastor, sir, and God has given you great grace, but you are in adultery and you need to repent. You are having an affair with a woman in your church.'

'How dare you accuse me!' the man stammered, standing with his arms folded.

Des turned away from the man and pointed at a woman in the congregation. 'Lady, you are from the same town, and you are the one he is having an affair with. Is that not true?'

The woman immediately broke down in tears. 'Yes, it's true,' she managed to say. 'The Lord have mercy on me!'

The crowd was astounded, but Des was not finished, as he picked out more people, exposing their hypocrisy. Then he gave an altar call.

'You have got one minute to get up to the front and repent,' he said. 'And if you don't, God will confront you and reveal your sin. You need to come now!'

165

Most of the crowd – 2,500 people – came running to the front.

'You cannot be saved if you have hatred in your heart for your brother,' Des told the people who had come forward, 'and people of other races are your brothers in Christ.

'You cannot say you love the Lord and yet hate your fellow man. Otherwise the love of God is not within you and you need to repent.

'Racism is a state of pride and an area of your hearts that you haven't yielded to God. But Jesus, through the cross, has made all men equal, and He doesn't look at the outward appearance, He looks at the inward appearance. Our sinful nature judges people on the outside, but God looks at the heart.

'All men are created in God's image – it doesn't matter what colour their skin happens to be. All men are born in sin and share the same guilt. But God sent His Son to die for all people of all races, so we shouldn't be treating them any different. We should also be laying down our lives for them,' Des concluded.

Ros and Des then led the people who had come forward in a prayer of repentance and started laying hands on people to receive deliverance. God had moved in a sovereign way – a single service which was to change the destiny of a church denomination forever.

Following this, the pastors met to amend the church's constitution and they started to welcome people of different races. They also started to reach out into the community and extend a hand of friendship to disadvantaged people, implementing a number of humanitarian initiatives.

Only God can change people's hearts, and He had done a great miracle in this place. He had taken a proud and insular group and turned them into a warm and welcoming community. Those who previously had enforced division, He was now raising up to repair the breach.

Chapter 13

A Fate Worse than Death

SOUTH AFRICA/MOZAMBIQUE

To live life without having really lived... to live life afraid.

Over their ten years in Africa, the Sinclairs have learnt to live their lives to the full, not scared of dying for what they believe and constantly embracing the miracle-working God they serve.

Because of their obedience to the call, the Lord is using them powerfully to bring salvation, healing and deliverance to people around the world, and especially in Southern Africa, where the couple travel extensively, leading mass crusades where many are healed and set free.

The Sinclairs are also helping to restore law and order in South Africa, a country which has one of the highest crime rates in the world, and to bring a message of faith in a land where there is much fear.

During the past decade Des and Ros have faced many different obstacles, not only in their own lives, but in helping others to find breakthroughs. For instance, during the year 2000, when they were watching news reports of the flooding in Mozambique, the Lord clearly told them to reach out in this desperate situation.

At the time, the couple were closely associated with a ministry which had a mission station in Vilanculos, Mozambique, but which was struggling to find drivers to transport essential aid to this flood-stricken region. In normal circumstances the ministry could have flown supplies in, but due to the floods, they were unable to land their plane.

'Lord, please open doors for more organizations to help the people of Mozambique,' Des asked the Lord as he prayed for the disaster area.

'Well, what are *you* prepared to do about it?' came the unexpected answer.

'Well, what can I possibly do?'

'You could drive up a lorry full of supplies and get food to the people.'

'But Lord, that's not possible – some of the roads are washed away.'

'There is a way!' the Lord said to Des, revealing to him how he could avoid the impassable roads by travelling through Zimbabwe, 'and I will be with you.'

'Then Lord, I am believing for You to open the doors!' Des said, concluding the ongoing conversation in his mind.

'Often thoughts like these come into my mind,' Des says. 'They challenge me, and I know the Lord is speaking to me to take action. Sometimes it's that still, small voice; sometimes it's loud; but more often than not, it's just an inward impression that God is speaking to me and I need to be obedient.'

So Des and a Norwegian volunteer by the name of Finnove set off from Johannesburg with forty tons of food, tents and blankets, and headed north towards the Zimbabwe border post at Beit Bridge.

Travelling through Zimbabwe was uneventful, until the two men reached Mutare, the gateway to Mozambique, where they were delayed for a couple of days until their paperwork was cleared by customs.

During this time, as they camped out at the border, Des and Finnove were able to witness to other lorry drivers and many of the local community, including a number of prostitutes. It seemed as if God was making full use of the longer, roundabout route He had revealed to Des.

'I look at every situation as an opportunity,' says Des. 'Every delay, or obstacle in your way, can open doors for God to move and make a way for you, where there seems to be no way, if you keep your attitude right and keep your eyes on Him.'

While waiting for customs clearance, Des looked at the men sitting around doing nothing and realized this captive audience was a great opportunity to preach the Gospel. It was not surprising to him, then, that 550 people prayed a prayer of salvation. While he and Finnove waited patiently along with the other drivers, they led a revival on the side of the road!

Finally, the necessary clearance came through, and by now the devil must have been hopping mad. The two men then headed for Beira with much-needed aid, turning south towards Maputo and the Vilanculos area, the region hardest hit by the floods.

There were many 'Danger' signs along the road warning of flood damage and landmines, and there was a large police and army presence. 'You shouldn't go any further – it's too dangerous,' a police officer told Des at a roadblock. 'Parts of the road have been washed away and the floods may have dislodged landmines, so you proceed at your own risk.'

Des could see a number of the local people shovelling sand alongside an old tractor, as they built up part of the road that had been eroded by the floodwater.

'We have to get this aid through to the people who are suffering,' Des replied, and the officer reluctantly waved the lorry on.

At a top speed of thirty to forty miles per hour, Des and his Norwegian colleague were making very slow progress, but each mile was taking them closer to thousands of people who were desperately hungry and homeless.

'At one time, it took us several hours to drive just sixty miles,' Des recalls, as they dodged huge potholes in the road, some of them resembling large craters. Often they came to a complete standstill to avoid goats and cattle and people walking in the road.

'You shouldn't go any further,' a Mozambican policeman told Des at another checkpoint, switching from Portuguese and trying to make himself understood in broken English. 'This area was heavily mined in the war and many of the mines have not been deactivated. Do you see how much of the land has been moved? If you go any further, you may hit a landmine.'

'We can't turn back now,' Des answered, but they stopped to rest and he and Finnove began to pray fervently about the whole situation. Both felt that the Lord was leading them to continue and that He would be with them.

By now Des and Finnove were being followed by a convoy of other vehicles travelling in their tracks, using the lorry as a buffer against potential disaster.

Then all of a sudden, Des felt the truck go into a slide, as if the road had disappeared beneath them. 'This is it,' he thought to himself. 'The lorry's going to roll!' But it didn't

– they just continued to slide through the sand, with the wheels on one side of the vehicle in mid air. It all happened in a split second, yet it seemed like an eternity. Des called out to the Lord, and the wheels returned to the ground and the truck regained its balance.

The next moment there was an enormous explosion as the Nissan pick-up which was following them disappeared in a mass of flames and a cloud of smoke. Des stopped his vehicle immediately, but there was nothing they could do. The pick-up had obviously hit a landmine and had been blown to bits, and many precious lives had been lost.

'Oh, Lord, I hope those men were saved!' Des prayed, asking for God's mercy to be upon them, as tears streamed down Finnove's cheeks.

The two men had witnessed a cruel disaster, but the Lord had supernaturally spared their lives and the lives of many others, since the much-needed supplies could so easily have been blown to bits.

How does one proceed on a journey after a shock like this? But the two men began to rejoice in the Lord's protection. 'We knew God was with us, because we realized we should have been the ones who were blown up,' Des recalls. 'But God had intervened on our behalf and we had a peace that He would continue to watch over us so that we could reach our destination.'

'We always pray over our vehicle when we travel,' says Ros, 'that the Lord would protect us, and for angels to be encamped around us.'

'And we dedicate the vehicle and the goods we are carrying to the Lord,' says Des, 'because we are firm believers that the Lord protects what belongs to Him.'

They still had to drive for another fifteen hours. Finally, after several days of travelling, Des and Finnove arrived in Vilanculos, where they were shocked to see how much of the land had been consumed by water.

But nothing could dampen the welcome they received as the mission staff rejoiced with them on their safe arrival and the flood survivors gathered to receive their first decent meal in a long time.

'You could see how distressed the people were,' Des recalls. 'Many of them had lost their homes and they had nothing left. Worse still, some had relatives who had drowned and many children were missing.

'It was a privilege to be able to help unload the lorry and give people fresh clothes and set up tents for those whose homes had been washed away, and of course, to share the Gospel with them.

'In a disaster like this, people are more open to the Gospel, as they look for answers, and we were delighted to find a local pastor who could speak sufficient English to act as an interpreter, so we were able to minister to the people and pray for hundreds to receive Christ.

'It was a real faith-building experience, and as the Lord promised, He was with us.'

Des has been back to Mozambique a number of times since then on various mercy missions, including a trip in September 2000, when he encountered another of this region's major dangers – malaria.

This time he was visiting a mission station in Pambarra, when he prayed for two young boys who had suddenly taken ill with cerebral malaria, a very serious strain of the disease, which can cause brain damage and is often fatal.

The boys were only three and four-years-old respectively, and both had a high fever and were dehydrated. A doctor advised their parents, Peter and

Belinda, to take them back to South Africa immediately for urgent medical care, but the parents were also coming down with the dreaded condition and soon became delirious and unable to care for their children.

And so Des and a medic named Billy stayed up throughout the night, praying for the boys and laying hands on them. They also had to bathe them constantly to keep their temperatures down, and try to force fluids down their throats, as they were both so dehydrated.

'It was a long and emotional night,' Des recalls, 'because I knew that if the Lord did not come through for these little boys, then by the morning they would be dead. I have rarely prayed and cried out to the Lord in such desperation.'

At about three o'clock in the morning, Brendan, the youngest boy, went into convulsions. Tears filled Des's eyes as he watched the little boy stop breathing.

'Why is this happening, Lord?' Des questioned. 'Your Word says that if we pray for the sick, they will be healed. Why have You left us?'

'I have not left you,' came the reassuring voice of the Lord, in immediate reply. 'Place your mouth over the young boy's mouth and breathe life into him seven times, and he shall be made whole. Then speak words of life over him.'

Des immediately started artificial resuscitation on the child. 'How's he doing?' he asked Billy. 'Is there any change?'

'It's too late,' the medic replied. 'He hasn't been breathing for over five minutes now.'

But just then, little Brendan started coughing, and began to breathe normally. Within the next hour his temperature returned to normal.

'This was one of the most amazing miracles I've ever

seen,' Des remembers today. 'God not only intervened in little Brendan's life, but later that morning he and his brother were both up and about, running around with their puppy – the symptoms of the malaria completely gone! It was absolutely wonderful to see such a great miracle of God's faithfulness in touching these young boys' lives. It was an awesome testimony which still inspires me today.'

Chapter 14

The Blood of the Martyrs Cries Out

HEAVEN (PART 3) AND HELL

'What have you done with My son?'

Angels have often made an appearance in the ministry of Des and Ros Sinclair, intervening many times to see the will of God carried out in their lives. Des remembers seeing heavenly beings during his divine revelation of heaven in 1987. He saw at first hand how the angels of the Lord are ministering spirits sent to do the will of the Father, and the Lord revealed something to him that was quite extraordinary...

'There is something important I want to show you,' the Lord said to Des as they walked up a large celestial corridor and into an enormous room.

Des was amazed. It was a nursery, and he was overwhelmed by the number of empty cots he saw of all different sizes. They were all on wheels, and one by one they were being pushed into queues as far as the eye could see.

'Lord, why are they queuing?' Des asked, studying the angelic figures pushing the cots towards what looked like an assembly line. They looked just like people, but they had large wings protruding from their backs.

'Come, let Me show you,' the Lord said, leading Des to the very front of one of the lines where the cots had stalled, waiting to receive something.

The next moment, a little baby appeared and the angel lovingly received it and placed it carefully into a cot.

Des watched as the process continued as, one after the other, more babies were received, put into cots and taken away. All of them looked so beautifully formed and healthy.

'Lord, where are all these babies coming from?' Des asked.

'I will show you,' the Lord said. 'Have a look into the tunnel.'

As Des leant over to put his head through, it seemed as though he had been whisked away, and the next minute he and the Lord were standing in a tunnel of light, looking down to earth. Moments later they were standing together in what looked like an operating theatre.

In the centre of the room, a woman was lying on a table, her large belly covered by a green cloth, but Des could see right through her to the life growing within her.

Here was a doctor who had taken an oath to protect life at all costs, yet he started to perform a procedure that was completely opposite to those noble beliefs.

Des listened sorrowfully as he heard the foetus screaming: 'Have mercy! Save me!' he heard it cry out, as he watched this delicate lifeform being ripped out of the apparent safety of its mother's womb.

blood scattered everywhere as it was torn out and put into a bag, discarded like a piece of rubbish.

'The blood of the martyrs cries out to Me,' said the Lord, comforting Des. 'I hear their cry.'

Then, in an instant, the hands of God reached down

into that bag and the Lord took hold of that child's spirit and embraced it. As the child's spirit left the earth, it was no longer a partially formed human being, but a fully developed baby and completely whole in the Father's presence.

'The blood of the martyrs cries out to Me,' the Lord said once again, 'but I hold them in My hands.'

And so the angels took these precious babies, who had died in this way, directly from the hands of Father God and placed them lovingly in their heavenly cots, to tend them with a love and compassion they had been denied on the earth.

'Let's go further,' said the Lord, leading Des through the nursery, which seemed to go on forever, but there were clearly different areas for different stages of growth.

In the first one, young babies were being cared for. In the next, Des was overjoyed to see the smiling faces of a great many toddlers as they crawled about in their heavenly playroom, lovingly cared for by angels.

In another area, the children were even more developed, running around and having fun. They were clearly growing up just like any child on earth. In another section, the older children were being nurtured and taught in the ways of the Lord.

Finally, they got to the teenage section, where Des was amazed to see a sixteen-year-old boy being embraced by his mother.

'You could hear exactly what was going on in her mind,' Des recalls. 'What I heard was this: she had become pregnant when she was a teenager and had aborted her baby, but now that she was in heaven, she was being reunited with her child. She had given her life to the Lord before she had died, and this sixteen-year-old was her aborted baby whom the Lord had raised.

'And what a joyful reunion, as the woman realized that the child she had mourned for had not been terminated as she thought, but was fully grown. What a joy to know that the Lord had seen her repentant heart and forgiven her, and she and her son now had the whole of eternity to catch up on what they had lost.'

Des was also amazed to see that the son clearly knew who his parents were and his whole family line, and there was such acceptance and belonging between him and his mother, like they had never been apart.

Des was overwhelmed by the goodness of God, when he realized that this was not an isolated incident – there were literally thousands of families waiting to be reunited with their children.

Of course, not all of these children were the victims of abortion. Some of them had been miscarried in pregnancy and others had been stillborn. Others had been stolen from their parents through cot deaths, or in various accidents, or through all kinds of diseases. But all of them had died in childhood and had been raised in this heavenly home, and it wasn't their past that mattered, only their future.

'Where are they going to?' Des asked as family after family passed by, celebrating their reunion.

'They are going to their mansion,' said the Lord, His eyes filled with mercy and compassion. 'I have prepared a home for them, where they will live in harmony forever with their child.'

Christians are not exempt from physical death, only spiritual death. Many beloved believers in Christ have been martyred in countries where false gods are served or a spirit of atheism exists, but always remember – the blood of the martyrs cries out to the Lord and He holds them in His hands.

In Des's heavenly experience, Jesus appeared to him as an ordinary man, though His eyes were filled with such love and compassion. Des knew the Lord could see straight through him, yet His eyes were not condemning, but rather reassuring and accepting.

He wore a white silk garment with gold embroidery around the collar, and at times, when the light caught His robe, you could see streaks of gold. And sometimes when Des looked at Him, it was as if the robe came alive and he could see things the Lord was showing him in picture format.

'Holy, Holy is the Lord God Almighty, who was and is and is to come,' Des could hear the angelic host singing. As he listened, it seemed the same question was continually being asked, followed by the same resounding answer:

'Who is worthy?' one choir of angels asked.

'He is worthy, the Lion of Judah has conquered. He alone is worthy,' another group answered, and so this divine interchange continued.

'Who is worthy to take the seal?'

'The Lamb of God, who takes away the sins of the world, He is worthy.'

The presence of the Lord was so overwhelming that Des fell down, his face prostrate to the ground. Then as he looked up, he could hardly move, as he saw a row of enormous feet.

These belonged to twenty-four massive beings seated on solid golden thrones, and were covered with golden sandals. In the centre of these thrones were three even larger thrones, almost eclipsed by the brilliant light emanating from them.

Standing behind each row of six thrones flanking the three middle thrones was a huge golden menorah. Each one had seven candles burning like fire.

The middle throne was so bright that Des couldn't look at it, but he caught a glimpse of two gigantic feet that looked like they were made from solid gold, and yet they looked like solid brass as well, and he saw that they could move.

'Lord, I cannot bear to be in the presence of Almighty God,' Des whispered to Jesus.

'You are here because I am with you,' Jesus answered.

The Lord was standing right next to him, but He was also sitting at the right hand of the Father in all His glory. To the left, the third throne was ablaze with a mass of flames, and Des could just make out the outline of a person who seemed to be consumed with fire.

The Lord led Des closer towards the largest throne, which had a golden altar in front of it. There, Des could see a lamb had been sacrificed, yet it was still alive and standing on the altar.

Its throat had been slit and there was a constant gush of blood streaming from it, down onto the altar and onto the floor, and flowing into what looked like a river of blood which divided the middle of this great throne-room. The blood covered the feet of the three enormous beings, gushing under their thrones.

'This is My blood,' the Lord said to Des. 'This is the blood that enables Me to plead on your behalf. This is the blood which allows Me to present your case before My Father.'

In Him we have redemption through His blood, the forgiveness of sins, according to the riches of His grace.

Ephesians 1:7

... you were not redeemed with corruptible things, like silver or gold... but with the precious blood of Christ, as of a lamb without blemish and without spot.

1 Peter 1:18–19

And they sang a new song, saying: 'You are worthy to take the scroll, and to open its seals; for You were slain, and have redeemed us to God by Your blood out of every tribe and tongue and people and nation.'

Revelation 5:9

As Des stood in the throne-room, a man was brought before the Lord by angelic guards covered in heavenly armour. The man immediately fell to the ground as the story of his life began to unfold before him. His selfish existence, his corrupt business dealings and the way he had mistreated others were revealed through a giant three-dimensional image more amazing than any movie screen Des had ever seen.

It was like an enormous video recording was being played back, showing the decisions the man had made and how he had rejected God in spite of all the times the Lord had intervened in his life. It became clear just how many opportunities he had been given to receive God's mercy, and how the Lord had answered his prayers on a number of occasions, and had sent people to share the Gospel with him, yet he had stubbornly refused to follow Jesus, no matter how much they had pleaded.

Des remembers looking at the Lord and seeing tears flowing from His eyes like a river, down His robe and covering the floor, as he heard a thunderous voice ask a simple question:

182

'What have you done with My Son?'

It was the unmistakable voice of the Father.

'Am I not the Lord God Almighty who is righteous and just? Yet why did you reject My Son? What do you have to say for yourself?'

The man cried out for forgiveness, pleading for mercy, but it was too late.

'Did I not show you My mercy, while you were on earth?' the Father asked. 'Many times I sent angels to protect you and healed you when you cried out to Me. I sent several people to speak to you and many times I tried to warn you, but you wouldn't listen. You stubbornly refused to acknowledge Me. Now your life is finished, and you must go to the eternity you have chosen. Now go.'

Des watched as the man was led away by the angels, kicking and screaming. Then he saw a vast door open which God Almighty alone could open or close, and he knew it was the gateway to hell.

As the door opened, Des could see a number of demonic creatures hovering around the threshold, but worse still, he could hear the anguish of millions of screams that seemed to cut to the very core of his being.

As Des looked through the door, he could see two guards standing in front of a dark tunnel, which seemed to be on fire, yet the flames gave no light. They had piercing red eyes and looked like men, yet they had no flesh on them.

As the angels let go of the man, it was as if he was automatically transported through the doorway and grabbed by a horde of demons, laughing and screaming. 'This is where you belong – you are our slave now!' they tormented him with an evil delight.

The man's flesh began to melt in the heat, and Des

could see his bones sticking through – a horrific picture of mutilation he could hardly describe. Then the doors closed and the man was gone forever.

At this point, Des, like the Lord Jesus, was also overcome with tears, as he mourned for all those he knew who had gone to a lost eternity. This was no isolated incident. The queue stretched for miles as, one by one, those who had rejected Jesus on earth faced the Father and received His judgment according to His Word.

'The wages of sin is death,' Des remembered, 'but the gift of God is eternal life in Christ Jesus our Lord' (Romans 6:23).

'Come, I still have much to show you,' said the Lord as he led Des down a dark passageway onto a rocky pathway close to the edge of a cliff. A sea of darkness seemed to engulf them, even though flames were coming up from a vast ravine below. As Des looked down, he could see rivers of molten lava flowing beneath them. Fires were raging everywhere, and yet he could hardly see in the pitch black.

As he and the Lord continued to walk, deformed beings began to appear in front of them, immediately bowing low before Jesus as He passed, and screaming out to Him for mercy.

'Get me out of here!'

'Don't leave me here!'

'Help me!'

And so the screams continued from every angle as Des tried to study the outline of the tragic figures in the dark. Their bodies seemed to be continuously melting, with masses of skin hanging off their bones, but it was the putrid smell of rotting flesh that drove home to him the extent of their suffering.

'I can't take this torment any longer,' he cried to the

Lord. Not only was he experiencing the utter despair of others, but he began to regret everything he had done in his life that was wrong, and all the times he had disobeyed the Lord and done things for his own gain.

'Lord get me out of here!' he cried once again, as guilt, condemnation and shame began to overshadow him. 'Lord, have mercy! I cannot bear this any more.'

'I have one more thing to show you here,' the Lord said as He stopped and laid His hand on the rock-face. All of a sudden the rock became transparent, like a wall of thick glass, and Des could see a countless mass of people trapped behind it.

They seemed to be standing in molten lava, their bodies on fire and their flesh perpetually melting, yet they were alive. When they saw Des, many of them ran up to the transparent wall of rock, scraping their fingernails against it in despair.

They were trying to get out and were screaming at him. Somehow Des knew exactly what they were trying to say, even though there were so many voices crying out at once. 'You must go back and tell the world that hell is a real place,' was their message. 'Go back and tell them what you have seen so that no more people will come here!'

Des looked at Jesus. 'Can't you do something?' he asked.

Tears gushed from the Lord's eyes, forming a pool of water at his feet. 'I have done all I could for them,' Jesus replied, as the colour of his tears changed to a bright red, and blood started to flow from His eyes. 'I shed My blood for them, and they rejected it. There is nothing more I can do. It is finished.'

Looking back on this horrific experience, Des is convinced that every Christian should have an understanding of the reality of hell, because if they don't know what they are saved from, they will not know what they have been given.

'If you know what hell is, you will be motivated to serve the Lord and preach the Gospel,' he says today, 'not out of fear, but out of love for all those you come into contact with. A divine revelation of hell motivates us to be obedient to the Lord and to fulfil the great commission He has given us, to go into all the world and share the Gospel with all people.

'The blood of the Lord Jesus still cries out today, offering the world the only escape from the horrors that face them, if they choose to deny the one and only Saviour and go their own way. How can they reject such great salvation?'

The Lord had shown Des many things, including a horrific insight into hell, and just as he thought he could take it no more, in the twinkling of an eye, they were out of that dark world, and back in the light where the incredible brilliance of the Father's presence illuminated the whole of heaven.

Then the Lord gave Des a picture of Africa, where he saw a crowd of thousands of people, like the sea of people he had been shown in heaven. Des could see a platform set up on a dusty, makeshift crusade ground, with two huge sound towers on each side. He was standing on the stage and he could hear himself preaching, his voice being amplified by the speakers to a mass of people.

Yet Des was not alone. The Lord was standing right next to him, the whole time he was preaching.

'Lord, you are with me!' Des said.

'Yes, I will be with you as you preach the Gospel throughout Africa, just I have shown you now. You will come to this place and many will be saved in My name. Now give a salvation call.'

And so Des obeyed, and as he began to give people an opportunity to receive Jesus as their Lord and Saviour, he saw the Holy Spirit descend upon the crowd with tongues of fire, and thousands of people started coming forward, falling on their faces before God and crying out before Him.

'Now lead them in prayer,' the Lord instructed.

The sound of so many people praying together was thunderous, and as they repented and accepted Christ into their lives, great rejoicing broke out amongst the angelic host.

'Today you have seen what brings Me glory,' said the Lord. 'Today you have seen the hand of darkness destroyed through My blood. We have brought thousands of people into My Kingdom. This is what brings Me glory!'

Chapter 15

You Will Stand Before Kings

SOUTH AMERICA

Do you see a man who excels in his work? He will stand before kings; he will not stand before unknown men.

Proverbs 22:29

During this experience of heaven and hell, Des had learnt a great many things, and the Lord had shown him thousands of people gathered to hear him preach, and that he would minister to presidents and kings.

Years later, this prophetic blueprint for his life continues to unroll as Jesus said it would. 'I will raise you up and you will be a prophet-evangelist to the nations of the world,' the Lord had told him during his out-of-the-body experience in Hamilton Hospital in New Zealand. 'You will go from place to place, you will sit at the feet of kings and proclaim My glory to them.'

Now the Lord was about to thrust Des into another potentially disastrous situation, which would bring him face to face with the president of a powerful South American country – and, if he didn't deliver, he would be back behind bars for the sake of the Gospel.

Des had been ministering in a church in Pretoria when the Lord gave him a word of knowledge for one of the men in the congregation, who walked with a limp and was facing a hip-replacement operation.

'God has heard your cry,' Des said. 'You have been asking the Lord to heal you and have been faithful, and God is going to heal your hip.'

A short while later, Des received a call. 'Do you know who I am?' the man asked.

'No,' answered Des, trying to recognize his voice.

'My name is Orvaldo and you prayed for me in Pretoria. You told me that God had heard my cry and was going to heal me. I just want to confirm to you that my hip is completely healed!' the man shared jubilantly.

'I have never experienced anything like this,' continued the man. 'All of sudden, it was like a fire touched the side of my leg and went into my hip, and the pain left me. And for the next twelve hours I had a warm feeling all over my body.

'One of my legs was shorter than the other, because my hip was breaking down, but now my legs are equal in length, and I no longer walk with a limp, and I have no pain!

'I went to the doctors and they told me they could not explain my recovery, but they said I was fine and no longer needed a hip-replacement operation.'

'Praise the Lord!' Des said. 'This is a wonderful testimony indeed. By the way, where are you from,' he asked, picking up that he had a foreign accent, 'and what do you do?'

'I am from South America,' Orvaldo answered. 'I am a diplomat, on the staff of my country's embassy here in Pretoria. Perhaps one day you will come and minister in my nation.'

Six months later Des got another call from Orvaldo, inviting him to the embassy. 'Our vice president is coming to South Africa and I would like to invite you to come and meet him and have lunch with us. Would you come?'

Des heard the Lord confirm that he should go: 'This is a divine connection that I have given you, but it is for an appointed time.'

So Des visited the embassy and listened politely as Orvaldo shared his testimony with the vice president. 'God is real, Mr Vice President. I know this first hand because He has healed me, and this is the man who prayed for me in my church.'

This gave Des an opening to share about Life Evangelism International's work in Africa and about some of the miraculous healings that Des and Ros had witnessed. He also began to minister in the word of knowledge, sharing many things about the Vice President's life and family, as the Spirit of the Lord came upon him and tears filled his eyes.

'How do you know that? Only God could know that! Please pray for me. I am a wicked man. I need Jesus.'

So Des was able to lead the Vice President in a salvation prayer, and he also prayed for him and his wife and family.

'You must come to South America,' said the Vice President. 'My people need to hear this and experience the true power of the Gospel. All we really know is traditional religion, and we do not see the power that you speak about. I will invite you.'

True to the vice president's word, Des later received an invitation to visit a country in South America (which cannot be named here, in order to protect the identity of a president who is still in office).

'At first I was very excited,' Des recalls, 'as I always had a passion to go to South America and minister there.

I was ready to book my ticket immediately and go, but the Lord kept showing us it was not His timing.'

When he talked to Ros about it and they prayed together, the answer was clear. 'No! Now is not the right time.'

'But why?' Des questioned the Lord. 'There are millions of people in South America who have never heard the Gospel and who are dying without an opportunity to be saved.'

'Because I have an appointed time for you, and if you go now, you will not achieve what I have called you do to,' the Lord answered. 'Be patient and wait, and I will tell you when the time is right. And when you go, you will change the destiny of a nation and bring release to the Church.'

Three years later, Des received an email from Orvaldo, asking him to pray for his country, which was about to hold an election. 'I am concerned that there is going to be a change in our government and that our new president could be a Communist,' Orvaldo wrote. 'It looks like the nation is going to vote a new party into power, whose leader has been trained by the Cubans. If they do, then we are in major trouble.'

As Ros and Des prayed about the situation, the Lord showed them that what Orvaldo feared was exactly what would happen and that Des's time to visit South America had arrived.

'Please come now,' the third invitation read. 'We need your help, because the newly elected president is trying to pass a law in Parliament that will outlaw all the Protestant churches in our country.'

As Des read this, God immediately quickened his spirit, and he remembered what the Lord had told him three years ago. 'Now is the appointed time,' the Holy Spirit revealed to Des. 'Now I want you to go.'

Des and Ros were so excited that this opportunity to minister overseas was finally coming to fruition. But there was a problem: they didn't have the money to buy the air-ticket.

'Lord, I'll go,' Des prayed, 'but you will have to provide a way.'

Less than an hour later, he received a phone call from some friends in Norway, Mike and Marit, who knew nothing about the South American opportunity. 'God has just spoken to me,' Mike said. 'God told me that He wants you to go to South America, and you need an airline ticket, and I'm transferring the money now.'

Ros and Des were astounded at this direct confirmation. Now they knew the Lord was about to do something amazing.

God's favour seemed to flow relentlessly from the moment Des arrived in the capital city for his two-and-a-half-month visit. 'We have arranged for you to address Parliament,' his host said. 'We would like you to give an explanation of how God can bless a nation and turn it around, or take His hand off a nation which does not honour Him. Please tell our government how God can bless a land and bring rain, or withhold the rain if we disregard Him, and how the land can become barren.'

Des was quite nervous about speaking to the Government, particularly on a subject that he did not know much about, other than what the Bible had taught him. But he agreed to go ahead, trusting the Lord for boldness and wisdom.

He was supposed to talk for twenty-five minutes, but ended up sharing with the government leaders for four and a half hours. Des had been praying and fasting and asking the Lord to move, and pretty soon his carefully orchestrated address became a full-on preaching session, as if he were at a crusade.

Des began to share the power of the Gospel, bringing in appropriate testimonies as the Lord led him. He shared how God would bless a land if the government applied godly principles, but how the Lord's judgement would come against a nation if it rejected God.

As he spoke, his words were simultaneously translated so that everyone present could understand what he was saying. Then, Des felt the liberty to issue the leaders with a challenge, and gave an altar call.

There, in the nation's Parliament and much to Des's joy, twelve members of the Communist party came forward to receive Jesus. They had tears in their eyes as they knelt before Des and he led them to the Lord.

When Des was finished, the President came up to him and started speaking to him through an interpreter, as he couldn't speak much English. 'Very powerful magic,' he said, 'to put people into a trance – but I am not a fool. You cannot persuade me like this. I am a Communist leader and you oppose everything I believe in.

'Why should I accept what you say? You come into my Parliament and preach everything my party stands against. If your God is truly alive, then prove it. I want you to gather all the Protestant churches together so I can see the power of your God.

'But if your God does not show up, I will put you in jail because you are a fraud. You had better be able to prove what you have done here today, or I will lock you behind bars.'

This was not unlike the challenge Des had faced from the Islamists who had gatecrashed his church service in Ghana, demanding that he raise their dead brother. This was certainly not an opportunity Des was about to give up on.

'Lord, You are able,' he thought to himself, and so through the President's aides, a mass meeting was hastily arranged for Christians of different denominations to gather on the fields outside the Parliament buildings.

Des structured the meeting as a day of prayer for the nation, and a stage was set up with sound towers and all the necessary facilities for a mass crusade – unbelievably, all at the government's expense!

When the day of the crusade came, many government leaders, including the President, were seated on the platform overlooking a crowd of some 800,000 people.

To start off, pastors of different denominations led prayers for God's blessing to fall; for the new president and all in authority; and for rain to fall in the drought-stricken northern region of the country.

Finally, it was Des's time to get up and preach the Gospel, and as he began to pray for the sick, people began to be healed all over the crowd. 'There are many blind people here, and others who are disabled,' Des said to the crowd. 'Where are you? I want you to come up onto the platform, so I can pray for you.'

The pastors started bringing people up onto the stage. The first man to come was pushing himself along on a makeshift trolley. His legs were obviously deformed and paralysed. He was completely unable to move his legs, let alone walk.

'Get the President to come and stand next to you,' the Lord instructed Des.

The nation's leader came over to Des, almost laughing at him in scorn. 'Your magic can't help this man,' he said.

'Wait and see,' Des replied. 'Do you acknowledge that this man is severely disabled and cannot walk?'

The president's aides tried to lift the man up, but his legs were just dangling and everyone could see that his muscles had shrunk.

'Now watch and see,' Des said, as he began to pray for the man, his knees knocking a little as he thought of the prison cell the president had waiting for him. 'Lord, You are able,' he prayed under his breath.

'In the name of Jesus Christ of Nazareth, rise up and walk!' Des commanded. Immediately the man's legs started moving and straightened out in front of the president's eyes. Then he stood up, picked up his trolley and started running across the stage!

The president's eyes were almost popping out of his head, but he still wasn't convinced. 'Good magic,' was all he could say.

'Thank you, Lord!' Des exclaimed. 'Bring another person.'

A blind man was led towards Des and the president. Des was shocked to see that he had no eyes – just empty sockets. He had never seen anything.

Des could see that the president was excited. He was talking quickly in his own language and Des couldn't understand a word, but he perceived that the nation's leader considered this a worthy test.

'Now you've got the real thing,' said the president through the interpreter. 'What are you going to do now? Your magic cannot grow new eyes.'

'So you recognize that this man has no eyes,' Des said, insisting that the president put his fingers in the holes on

195

the man's face where his eyes should have been. A friend of the man testified that he had been born this way and had never seen the light of day.

'What can you do for him? Where is your God now?' the president taunted Des.

'I am going to pray for him,' Des said, 'because my Lord is here.'

Des closed his eyes as he started to pray, 'Lord, I know You can do anything and I thank You for healing the disabled man. But now, You are going to have to make new eyes for this blind man. Show us Your glory, Lord! Show us Your power!'

'I must admit, I was reluctant to open my eyes,' Des recalls, 'in case I still saw empty sockets, but all of a sudden the crowd went crazy. All I could hear was a great noise, and as I opened my eyes, I could see the man touching the president's beard with great fascination. He didn't know who the person in front of him was. He had never seen a man before, and was closely examining the president's face, which was why the crowd had erupted.'

Des went up to the man to see what had happened, and rejoiced as he saw that the Lord had given him new eyes! The man was amazed as he continued to look around and touch things he was seeing for the first time.

The president was clearly shaken. 'Now you know that Jesus Christ is alive!' Des challenged him. 'You cannot deny that God is here by His Spirit.'

'I can't breathe,' the president replied, not understanding that the anointing was so strong on the platform that he could no longer stand in the presence of God. 'I cannot explain this any more,' he said to his aides as they whisked him away.

Meanwhile, back in South Africa, Ros, who was fasting

and praying for the meeting, was overjoyed to hear reports from Des of all that was going on. 'My constant prayer for my husband is that the Lord would fill him with the Holy Spirit and give him the very words he needs to speak, that God's light will shine through him to the people, in keeping with Isaiah 60:1, drawing them out of the darkness, and that the Holy Spirit would radiate powerfully through Des to the people, drawing them to God.'

A few days after the mass meeting, Des was summoned to attend a meeting at the president's office, which was a bit of a worry for his Christian hosts, as they feared the Communist leader's retaliation.

'You could be in a great deal of danger,' Des was cautioned, 'but all the Christians in the nation are praying for you.' For Des, it was just another opportunity to reach out to this man, and so he agreed to go.

'Just keep everything very simple,' was another piece of advice that was to prove valuable. 'The President is an uneducated man, so don't give him long, drawn-out explanations.'

Once again, there was a flurry of government officials and presidential aides as Des was welcomed into the leader's office.

'What I experienced at the church gathering, I cannot explain,' the president began, speaking through an interpreter. 'There was such an overwhelming power. How do you explain this?'

'It was the presence of God,' Des replied, trying to be as concise as possible, 'reaching out in love to all men, not to condemn us or destroy us but to show us that God is with us and He loves us.

'Just so that you know that God is real, and what you saw was from God, I want to tell you that the Lord knows

197

the condition you have,' Des said as he began to minister in the word of knowledge.

'You are planning a trip to the USA to meet President Bush for the first time,' Des said, as the leader looked at him incredulously.

The South American leader began shouting at his aides.

'He wants to know how our security has been breached,' the interpreter said.

'How do you know this?' the president then asked through the interpreter. 'Nobody knows of my plans.'

'God told me,' Des answered. 'He knows all things, and furthermore, while you are in the States, you are booked into clinics for treatment of a hereditary condition in your bone marrow.

'In fact, doctors are telling you that your back may need to be pinned to stop your spine from bending, and if it carries on, you may end up in a wheelchair. Is this not true?'

'How do you know this?' the President shouted angrily. 'Only my doctors know this. But this is all true.'

'Can I pray for you?' Des asked. 'God knows your condition, and it is He who has revealed it to me, because He wants to heal you from it.'

'You come in here and tell me these things, and I don't know whether you are a spy or whether I have a leak in my security,' replied the President, 'but I am going to pursue all avenues. I will find the leak and who has told you this. But just so I cover all angles, you can pray for me.'

So Des prayed for the president, breaking that genetic curse over his family in the name of Jesus and speaking life into his bone marrow and spinal cord.

'You also have gallstones,' Des ministered further, 'and you are booked in to have them laser treated.'

This made the President even more furious as he contemplated the depth of his security breach. 'Yes, I have been told that is the best way to treat them, rather than operating. How do you know this?'

'God told me!'

'Well, whatever. I will get to the bottom of this!'

As Des continued to pray for him, the president collapsed into his seat as if he was in a drunken state and started to laugh. This unnerved his bodyguards, as they hadn't heard him laugh before.

'You must go now,' one of the guards insisted, quickly ushering Des out.

After this, Des continued to minister in mass crusades across the nation, leading believers in prayer that the bill to ban all Protestant churches would be thrown out of Parliament.

A number of weeks later, once the president had returned from the United States, he requested to see Des again.

'What happened in the USA, Sir?' Des asked, once they had exchanged pleasantries. 'Did they operate on you?'

'No, they didn't. They first did DNA testing and took bone-marrow specimens. Then later, when they checked my back, they said it had straightened out perfectly and that I no longer have a bone-marrow condition.

'Then, when they examined me for gallstones, but they found none. You cannot believe the Americans – they will tell you anything – but according to them, I no longer have these conditions. So it was a waste of time and money to go there,' he concluded with a laugh.

'Well, Sir, I believe that God is speaking to you and that He sent me to tell you not to pass this anti-Protestant law. Do not do this, for if you do, it will bring destruction on your nation and it will be your downfall.

'You need to repent and receive Jesus as your Lord and Saviour,' Des challenged the president, despite warnings from his officials that he could be thrown into jail if he tried, but he felt a liberty in the Spirit to do so.

At this stage the president asked his security guards to leave, keeping only one interpreter with them. Then, shaking his head profusely, he stared at Des with tears in his eyes. 'I cannot deny what I have experienced, and that God is speaking to me, and because of all these things I will drop the bill.'

'But it is more than that, Sir,' Des replied. 'You can lose your soul. You need to make a choice to serve Jesus.'

'I am not ready to make a call like that, because if I do, I will have to step down, as I will no longer be a Communist. But you are welcome to come back to my country any time.'

And so, through a series of divine interventions, God turned a modern-day king's heart around, using a young evangelist who dared to step out in faith and put his life on the life for the Gospel.

Not only was the anti-Protestant bill thrown out, but the president later passed legislation to allow funding for Protestant organizations to undertake development projects.

Now thanks be to God who always leads us in triumph in Christ, and through us diffuses the fragrance of His knowledge in every place.

2 Corinthians 2:14

Chapter 16

Behold, I Give You Power

'Behold, I give you the authority to trample on serpents and scorpions, and over all the power of the enemy.'

Luke 10:19

Des woke up with a jolt. A hot, searing pain was shooting through his leg. 'Ros!' he yelled out, 'Something's bitten me!'

His wife looked back at him in horror as Des scrambled to his feet. A long, dark snake she did not recognize was slithering away into the Zimbabwean bushveld.

Ros quickly examined his leg. Indeed, there were two bite marks on his foot. It was the worst pain Des had ever experienced. It felt as if a fiery skewer had been thrust into his leg, setting his whole body aflame. His leg started to swell and he broke out in a sweat. His head was spinning and his body shaking.

Ros cried out to the Lord, as some of the local people came running towards them to see what the commotion was all about. 'You're a dead man, boss!' one of the men shouted. 'I saw the snake – it is very dangerous.'

Ros and Des had been travelling most of the night. They had left their home in Johannesburg at midnight to

201

reach the Beit Bridge border post early the next morning before the influx of traffic. They were on their way to Harare, the capital of Zimbabwe, to preach at a tent crusade and a pastor's conference and had stopped at the Bube River service station to rest.

Exhausted from driving, Des had lain down under the shade of some trees in the front of the service station. It was good to doze in the shade – until disaster struck.

'What do you mean?' Des asked the man, trying to talk above the pain.

'Black mamba, boss,' the petrol attendant answered. 'I saw it come and bite you and run away. You are a dead man.'

'How do you know it's a mamba?' Des asked.

'Mambas live here,' the attendant answered. 'This is mamba country.'

Des motioned to the attendant and some of the locals to find the snake to make sure, but they were too scared. A couple of men wandered off into the bush to have a look, and as soon as they saw it, there was no question what type of snake it was.

The mamba had reared a third of its body off the ground, and was in its characteristic striking position – neck flattened, hissing very loudly and displaying its distinctive inky black mouth and deadly fangs.

Needless to say, the men did not stick around and made a dash back to the safety of the filling station.

'It is definitely a black mamba, boss,' one of them confirmed.

'Do you have the antidote in the petrol station?' Ros pleaded. 'What must we do? Tell us quickly!'

'We have no serum,' the attendant answered. 'Sorry, madam – he is a dead man.'

It was as if a fire was raging within Des, but he was not about to give up, and started quoting Scripture. 'Lord, Your Word says You have given me authority to trample on snakes and scorpions, and overcome all the power of the enemy, and nothing shall harm me!' he cried out, examining his leg.

'Lord, in the name of Jesus Christ, I proclaim this Scripture over this situation, and through the blood of Jesus I pray this venom will not have power over me, but rather Your blood will destroy the power of the evil one,' he managed to say in front of the people gathered around him, as Ros laid hands on the two-pronged bite.

She was also praying under her breath and believing God for a complete healing. 'Lord, I pray for Des, that you will restore his strength and deliver him out of the snare of the enemy.'

Then she got angry with the devil and addressed him directly. 'How dare you, Satan? How dare you try to stop us from preaching the Word of God in Zimbabwe, to those who do not know the power of the Gospel. I break your power over Des's body and through the blood of Jesus, I command his body to come into line, in Jesus' name.'

A million thoughts were going through her mind as she looked into her husband's pained eyes. Unlike some women, who would have fallen apart in such a crisis, she remained calm and circumspect, with an inner strength and peace gleaned from years of seeing God come through for her in the worst of circumstances.

Des also began to take authority over Satan's hold on this entire situation. 'Devil, I break your power over this condition in the name of Jesus and I command you to leave, right now!' he declared.

Des also continued to cry out before the Lord: 'Father,

You know I am on the way to Harare to preach the Gospel. I'm here in Your name. You have sent me here to preach Your Word. The devil has tried to stop me, and I take authority over this in the name of Jesus!'

When Ros and Des are faced with challenges and obstacles such as this, Ros is not one to get hysterical. 'I immediately switch over into prayer mode and trust the Lord for His divine intervention,' she says.

Clearly, the Lord had hand-picked the right wife for Des – someone who could cope with all the challenges they have had to face together, a prayer warrior who, many times, has helped keep her husband alive through her ongoing intercession, and at times, her intense spiritual warfare.

'I knew that God had called us to preach in Zimbabwe,' Ros recalls, 'and that this incident was the devil trying to stop us from getting to our preaching engagements, just like he had conspired to wipe my parents out in this same country years before. And so I became very angry with the evil one.

'We were in the middle of nowhere, right out in the bush – all we could do was have faith in God, and I knew He would come through for us, as He always does!

'It was almost as if I rose up in a righteous anger, which gave me tremendous inner strength in the face of a seemingly impossible situation.'

The crowd were still watching Ros and Des intently. They could not believe he was still standing. 'Boss, aren't you feeling funny?' one of them asked.

'I'm feeling much better, actually,' Des replied as the people shook their heads in amazement.

Des knew that the black mamba is one of the deadliest snakes in the world and the largest venomous snake in

Africa. It seemed strange to him that the snake had attacked without provocation – he had been fast asleep when he was bitten. But snake experts have described mambas as the world's most aggressive snakes, noting their tendency to attack for no reason at all.

In addition, these fast-moving tree-snakes have an extremely potent neuro-toxic venom, which is said to have a nearly 100-percent fatality rate. It immediately attacks the nervous system, shutting down the lungs and heart. Less than two drops of it can kill a fully grown man unless the appropriate anti-venom is administered in time.

The Lord had so obviously delivered Des once again – literally from the jaws of death. The crowd were flabbergasted. What the devil had meant for evil, God was about to turn to good (see Romans 8:28). The crowd were hanging around, waiting for Des to die, but after half an hour, the pain seemed to have subsided and he felt much better.

'You're okay?' someone asked him, trying to work out what was going on. 'This is impossible – no man lives after a mamba bite. You should have been dead long ago. You can't be human – you must be superman!'

'That's right!' Des answered as the Lord started to whisper to him. 'I am not of this world, because I belong to Jesus Christ, and He is not of this world. It is through His power that the mamba bite has no authority over me.'

They looked at him in surprise and started to disperse.

'Where are you going?' Des asked.

'We must go and call the *sangoma* [witchdoctor],' somebody answered. 'He told us that our ancestors would come and show us their power, so maybe you are our ancestor. We must call him and our families to come and see.'

Ros and Des waited while a crowd from the nearby village formed, and finally the *sangoma* came. When he began to confirm that Des was indeed their ancestor, it was time for the young evangelist to silence this deception and start preaching the truth!

'It does not help you to worship your ancestors or sacrifice animals to them,' Des shared with them lovingly. 'There is only one true God and only one blood sacrifice that pleases Him – the blood of His Son, Jesus Christ.'

Des began to share in detail about the ultimate atonement and the power of the blood of Jesus Christ, which was more powerful than a mamba bite. 'The power of death has no power over the blood of Jesus, because the blood of Christ is life!' he said.

Then he began to pray for the sick, taking spittle and rubbing it on the eyes of a blind man. He told him to go and wash his eyes, and when he came back, the cataracts were completely gone and the man could see.

A demon began to manifest through the witchdoctor and he began to squirm on the ground like a snake, hissing at the crowd and coming towards Des, as if to attack him.

'In the name of Jesus Christ, I break Satan's hold over this man,' Des prayed, and the man immediately stopped in his tracks.

Des had already overcome the attack of a snake in the physical realm, and was not about to be cornered by one in the spiritual realm. It was time for the great serpent, Satan, to give up his hold and for his demonic cohorts to be cast out of this man's life, after years of torment.

It was also time for a whole community to see that the power of God was much stronger than the power of witchcraft. The man was now of a sound mind and able to listen to Des, who led him to the Lord.

Des's leg was still swelling up like a balloon, but he did not let that stop him, and for two hours he and Ros continued to pray for people as more and more villagers came forward for healing.

God had turned the whole situation around with a supernatural display of His great power, which had saved many lives, delivered a *sangoma* from his witchcraft and healed many people.

Des and Ros were very excited as they got back on the road to complete the four-hour journey to Harare. 'This is a good sign of what is to come, for our meetings,' Des said to Ros.

When they arrived at the pastor's house, where they were staying, he was amazed to hear what they had been through on their journey. 'Do you think I need to go to the hospital and have this bite checked out?' Des asked.

The pastor laughed. 'It has been many hours now. If you are not dead now, you never will be!

'What about my leg? It's all swollen up.'

'We'll pray for it again and see what it looks like tomorrow.'

When Des woke up the next morning, the swelling had almost completely gone and he was able to continue with the tent crusade and the pastor's conference he was preaching at, both of which turned out to be very successful.

'We have a saying: "The more Satan tries to throw at you beforehand, the better the meetings are going to be", and this was a perfect example of this in action,' Ros says. 'You are on the right track when the devil tries to attack you on every side, because he's running scared.

'We were so excited on our way to Harare that day,' she recalls, 'knowing the Lord had great things in store for us, because of the situation. We have learnt that when

Satan tries to throw stuff at you, that is the time to rejoice and press on and press through.'

The Sinclairs have since been on many different trips to Zimbabwe, ministering in all kinds of places, from little villages like Chegutu, through to the towns of KweKwe and Gweru and the city of Harare – and each trip has been a fulfilment of God's calling on Ros and her family.

What the devil had tried to steal from the Browns when Ros was a child, God has turned to good, through the ministry of Life Evangelism International today. She and Des have held many crusade meetings in Zimbabwe, and one region of the country where they have enjoyed tremendous success is the Musana rural area, where ancestral worship is prevalent.

'We went into this crusade praying against spirits of ancestral worship,' says Ros, 'that their stronghold over this community would be broken, and through the prayers of many people around the world, we saw the Lord move in a way that was nothing short of miraculous.

'One fifth of the rural population attended the crusade and approximately one sixth of the adults in the community made a commitment to the Lord. Even the twenty-four witchdoctors who had sat in the front row of the crusade meetings came up to receive salvation over several nights, and many miracles also occurred.'

On the second night of the Musana crusade, a sixty-three-year-old man was brought into the tent in a wheelbarrow. Unable to walk, he lay on a plank at the front of the crowd until after the message, when Des prayed over him.

God immediately healed the shrunken muscles in his legs, and he was able to get up onto his feet and march up and down in front of the tent. When the crowd saw this miracle, they were amazed and began to chant the name of Jesus. Many of them knew the man and how long he had suffered. Now they were shouting 'Jesus, Jesus, Jesus!'

'This was an amazing confirmation of the Lord Jesus' resurrection power,' Ros recalls, 'which Des had been preaching that night. This same man was not only healed and received Christ, but was later baptized in water and filled with the Holy Spirit – all in the space of a few days. His face absolutely glowed with transformation from God!'

Following this miracle, a number of other disabled people were healed during the meetings, with people leaving the crusade grounds carrying their walking sticks instead of hobbling along on them, their pain supernaturally gone in the wonderful name of Jesus.

'The truth of the resurrected, living Lord had gone forth into this community, not only in word but in great power, bringing spiritual breakthrough,' says Ros. 'Furthermore, charms, fetishes, *muti* and tools of the witchcraft trade were publicly burnt, bringing freedom to the captives.'

It is only through the higher power of the Gospel of Jesus Christ that those who are held in bondage by witchcraft can be set free, and this is something Ros and Des have seen many times in their lives, as the Lord gives them power to overcome the works of darkness.

Perhaps the most profound example of Des's run in with witchcraft came in Kaduna during his visit to West Africa, when he was invited to address a Gospel crusade in Nigeria.

'This is a major stronghold of witches,' the Lord warned Des as his plane left Ghana for Nigeria. 'Prepare yourself, because there will be much opposition against this crusade,' he felt the Lord say deep within his spirit. 'Be careful of a witch from America who will try to come against you. But do not be afraid – I will be with you.'

The pastors hosting Des were quick to confirm this when he arrived in Kaduna, as a large number of witchdoctors had been seen camping at the edges of the crusade ground and all kinds of evil artefacts had been found, including what looked like the remains of a human sacrifice.

World-renowned evangelist Reinhard Bonnke had recently completed a massive evangelistic campaign in the region, literally pushing back the gates of hell, and now the devil was bringing witches from all over West Africa to try to take back the ground they had lost.

'There has always been a lot of sorcery in our country,' said one of the pastors, 'but we have never seen such an increase in witchcraft. The police are very concerned and the Church is praying.'

On the first night of the crusade, just north of Lagos, the Lord moved sovereignly, with approximately 20,000 recorded converts and many healings. But on the second night, all hell broke loose.

While the worship team were leading the large crowd in a jubilant praise song, the crowd started to part in horror as a procession of evil forced its way through the people.

A group of thirteen witches were making their way to the front of the crowd, carrying a bamboo stretcher on their shoulders. Lying on top of the stretcher was the lifeless body of a young boy, whose throat appeared to have been slit.

'What are we going to do?' the pastor asked Des.

'Don't worry, the power of God is here,' Des answered confidently. 'Leave them. The Lord will deal with them...'

As Des got up to address the crowd, one of the witches pulled back her hood, revealing that she was white.

'This woman is one of the highest-ranking witches in the world,' the Lord spoke into Des's spirit. 'She has come here from California to try to overthrow this crusade. She is very strong, but she has no power over Me and she has no power over you, because I have defeated her at the cross.'

The American witch started to chant and point a stick into the crowd, causing people to fall over under the power of darkness.

'I rebuke you in the name of Jesus!' Des shouted at her, taking authority over this manifestation of evil.

The woman was incensed. She pointed her stick towards Des, and it started to grow, extending itself closer and closer towards the lectern from which he was preaching.

As the stick hit the top of the lectern and touched Des's Bible, it was as if a lightning bolt descended from heaven, and a visible current ran down the stick and hit the woman, throwing her up into the air and into the crowd, gasping for air.

'Lord, don't kill her – just save her!' Des prayed out loud.

The American witch hit the ground and lay there for a long time, unable to move. Many thought she was dead, she looked so lifeless.

Des proceeded to preach a powerful salvation message and gave an altar call for people to come forward to receive Jesus. At this time the woman was able to pick herself up out of the dust and come to the front, where she kneeled in repentance.

'I came here to kill you,' she cried, 'but I've seen a greater power at work and I want to surrender to the true God.'

The woman continued to confess how she had come over from the USA to cast spells against Des and the pastors hosting the crusade. The crowd gasped in horror as she gave details as to how she had presided over the human sacrifice of the young boy lying on the bamboo stretcher – how she had slit his throat and drained his blood.

Des prayed a powerful prayer of deliverance over the woman, casting out demons and setting her free in the name of Jesus. He then moved on to pray for many of the people who had come forward to receive salvation, not quite sure how to handle the problem of the dead child lying before him, his blood drained out of him.

'Lord, show Your glory!' Des started to pray passionately. 'If You can save this witch, You can save this child. Lord, please touch this young boy in the name of Jesus!'

The witches and witchdoctors surrounding the boy fell to the ground as the Lord started to move in great power, some of them coming to the front, pleading for mercy.

As Des started to lead them in prayers to break the curses over their lives, a great commotion broke loose across the crowd, as the young boy was brought back to life and was carried up onto the stage.

Without fanfare or pomp and ceremony, the Lord had resurrected him and his neck was completely healed. There wasn't even any evidence of a scar. Des hugged the little boy and prayed for him.

The witches had been about to set him on fire, but now he was able to watch his stretcher being burnt in a massive bonfire along with a large collection of witchcraft items that had been surrendered by the witches and members of the crowd.

What a crusade meeting! People went home rejoicing at all they had seen. In the face of a devilish showdown, God had clearly shown Himself to be an infinitely greater power.

'When the enemy comes in like a flood,' Des says, quoting Isaiah 59:19, 'the Spirit of the Lord will lift up a standard against him' and this is exactly what happened here. The God we serve is Almighty God and His power is greater than any other.'

It seems as if overcoming all the works of the evil one has become a lifetime occupation for the Sinclairs, yet they are no different to any other ministry couple who are passionate about God and seeing him work through their ministry. And they are convinced that the same supernatural protection afforded to them is available to all.

Chapter 17

God's Grace is Sufficient

SOUTH AFRICA

'No man, no devil, no sickness will take our lives until we have achieved all that God has set for us to do.'

Des and Ros Sinclair are very ordinary people who do not see themselves as anything special, except that they are sold out to God, completely reliant on His guidance and provision, and obedient to go anywhere He leads them and to do whatever He tells them.

Yes, there have been many great escapes and times of incredible protection from disaster. Yes, there have been amazing angelic appearances and phenomenal healings in their ministry, but this is purely by the grace of God. And for this Des and Ros give Him all the glory.

The Sinclairs haven't often shared these experiences in the past, and have been reluctant to record them in book format up until now, in case people would look to them, rather than to the Lord.

But they believe that God has now released them to do so, as a witness and a testimony to all He has done in their lives and to encourage fellow believers to trust God more deeply and step out and do more for Him.

Des and Ros have also made every effort to ensure that what has been recorded is not only accurate, but that each account captures some of their humanity as imperfect vessels in the service of the Master.

For just like any other believer, there have been difficulties to deal with in their personal lives as well disappointments and times of betrayal when people have let them down. One particular area Des has had to deal with has been his health.

He has had to watch what he eats and monitor his blood sugar, having been diagnosed with diabetes, a condition which humbles him daily.

God had supernaturally healed his back in the Olivedale Clinic, following what happened to him in Angola at the hands of ruthless rebel soldiers, and miraculously, he was able to walk again, in spite of what the doctors had told him. Yet he is still waiting for his pancreas to be completely healed.

Des has experienced partial healing, his doctors having expressed amazement at how well balanced his blood sugar is for a man who is not always able to eat exactly as he should, due to his hectic ministry schedule. And when Des is preaching in crusades across Africa, he finds that he doesn't need to take insulin at all, because God has supernaturally intervened.

Ironically, through Des's ministry, hundreds of diabetics have been healed, yet this is a condition he has to cope with and monitor on a regular basis when he is at home. At the time of writing, Ros and Des are still believing for a complete healing of this condition, in the full knowledge that God's grace is sufficient in each and every situation.

'It is not easy to cope in a situation like this, especially when you are a person of faith, preaching faith and praying for the sick in all your meetings,' says Des. 'I see hundreds of chronic diabetics being healed in my meetings regularly, as well as people with much worse conditions.

'Ros and I also receive reports, quite often, which have been sent to us from chronic diabetics whom we have prayed for, who have been completely healed. They may have been dependent on insulin for years, but following prayer, their sugar level has stabilized and their doctors have confirmed that they no longer need insulin, and they are writing to testify to what God has done in their lives and to thank us for praying for them.

'Many times, when you pray for people, you know when they are receiving from you and are being healed, and when this happens, the personal prayer in the back of my mind is, "Lord, I need some of that as well!"

'Living with diabetes is not easy. Your sugar level is up one minute and down the next, and you have to monitor it by pricking your fingers. Then you need to inject yourself with insulin to balance your blood sugar, and constantly watch what you eat. It also affects your emotions and your reasoning.

'It really is a battle to live with in many ways, and I am believing for the Lord to completely heal me. In the meantime, I am so aware of the Lord's faithfulness in helping me to effectively manage the situation, so I don't allow diabetes to affect me in any way.

'I will not allow the devil to use this, or anything else, for that matter, to hinder me. So while I realize I have to be responsible for my condition, and do the best I can, at the end of the day, I thank the Lord for the power of the cross and the blood of Jesus.

'And I give Him praise for healing every disease known to man, including diabetes, and I lay this condition at the cross. My confession is that I don't receive it, and I ask the Lord to cover it with His blood and keep my sugar level balanced so that I am able to carry out all the things that He has called me to do for His glory.'

Des finds that when he is ministering in a crusade, his blood sugar levels are near perfect and he doesn't need any insulin while he is under the anointing, which is amazing, given the remote places he visits to preach the Gospel, often far from medical care.

The reality is that he could go into a diabetic coma at any time, but he continues to go where God calls him, in blind obedience, trusting that the God who sends him to the mission-fields of Africa is well able to sustain him there. So the fact that Des is preaching the Gospel with this condition is a miracle.

Even so, some fellow ministers have told Des that he cannot possibly be a faith preacher with this condition – that he obviously has a lack of faith, and until God heals him, he has nothing to testify about.

Des disagrees. 'Everyone has challenges to face in their lives, all of which are very different, and while God's will is always to heal us, sickness can sometimes be the "thorn in our flesh" that we have to bear, just as the Apostle Paul had to.

'The important thing, though, is that we never use this as an excuse not to fulfil God's divine calling on our lives. We must not let it distract us from the great commission we have received to win souls.

'I believe Jesus came to give us life, and life in abundance, and paid the price for all known sicknesses, so we as God's servants in this hour cannot allow sickness to control us. So I don't receive diabetes, but I must be faithful to care for my physical body and preserve it, because it is the dwelling place of God's Spirit.

'It is only by God's grace that I am not dead. It is by His grace that He stabilizes my blood sugar, and even though I have to manually stabilize it through injections, He gives me the grace to do this.

'I am not a good diabetic – I don't always play strictly by the rules, I don't always eat perfectly on time, or the right foods, necessarily. Ministry doesn't always allow me to do this. If I did all these things by the book, I couldn't carry on in ministry.

'I put the work of the Lord first, and God intervenes. While many diabetics battle to keep their blood sugar level, doctors are amazed at how balanced mine is, and how well I am. It is only by the grace of the Lord that I can carry on – but then, God's grace is sufficient for every one of us, no matter what we may be facing, if we rely on Him.

'It is the sick who need a doctor,' Des says, referring to Mark 2:17, 'and that is why the Lord Jesus came. So I would encourage every sick person to be of good courage, and don't ever think that God has forgotten you. Rather, keep on believing for your miracle and don't allow your condition to hinder you from fulfilling God's call on your life, because the devil wants it to become a stumbling-block.

'If you let it stop you from praying for the sick and from carrying on in your call and in your life, then the devil has a stronghold over you and has muzzled you. On the contrary, be determined to press on and fulfil all that God has for you in your life. Trust the Lord, thank Him for your healing. But also thank Him for the grace to live a normal life, and take authority over your condition.'

God has preserved Des many times, and he refuses to allow this condition to stop him from going where the Lord tells him. To him and Ros, dealing with diabetes is nothing in comparison to some of the situations he has been through in his life.

'All believers face some danger,' says Des. 'Living in South Africa, you constantly hear stories of people who have been robbed or hijacked or have died from malaria. These things can very easily become a threat to people and stop them from going anywhere. I could easily use diabetes as an excuse, but I constantly remind myself that it is no longer I who live, but Christ lives in me. And no sickness, prison, man or devil can have authority over my life!'

Des recalls an incident which really made this clear to him while he was on a ministry trip in Europe. He was flying from London to Switzerland, and there was so much turbulence in the air that the plane began to shudder through the clouds, making it a very bumpy ride.

Then, while they were flying over the Alps, some of the passengers became very distressed, particularly a woman in the seat next to him, and he felt he had to try to calm her down. Though she was a rather prim and proper English woman, she started to panic and soon become hysterical. 'We're all going to die and I'm never going to see my grandchild! *Save me!*' she cried.

By now many of the other passengers were also becoming distraught, and Des had heard enough doubt and unbelief.

'Quieten down, lady!' he shouted.

She looked back at him, horrified.

'We're all going to die – at least you can be nice to me!'

'You're not going to die,' he said. 'There is no way that

this plane is going to crash while I am on board. The devil has no authority to take my life until I have fulfilled all that God has for me. So you'd better stay close to me, because if this plane goes down, I am getting off it, and if you stick with me, so are you!'

This is exactly how Des and Ros think in whatever situations they have to face. They have incredible insight into what God has called them to do, and amazing faith to see it accomplished. They empower as many others as they can as they journey together in God.

'It doesn't matter what we face,' says Ros. 'If Des is shoved in jail again without insulin, the fact is that God will intervene and save his life. No man, no devil, no sickness will take our lives until we have achieved all that God has set for us to do, and when we have achieved those things for His glory, then the day will come when the Lord will take us home – and what a great and glorious day that will be!

'We can't use sickness as a crutch, or as an excuse to hold back on the things of God and the call that is on our lives. No one individual is going to save the whole world. Neither does God put this kind of pressure on any one person. But He has given each and every one of us something in our hands, and the important thing is, what are we going to do with the opportunities and resources that He has provided?

'We are not called to do everything for God, but what we can do, we must do for Him. How awesome it is to know that God chooses simple people like ourselves to do His work, and His work is not a burden but a great blessing to us.

'Yes, Des and I have come all the way to Africa to help others, but what an impact Africa has had on our lives! For me personally, as a little country girl, my horizons have been broadened so much. I have come out of my shell like I would never have believed, and the Lord has put such a passion in our hearts for people.

'What we've experienced, we would not have any other way. If I could live my life over again, I would change nothing – even all the bad times, the hard times, the heartache, and the waiting, wondering if Des is dead or alive. I wouldn't change any of it, because there is nothing more fulfilling than being in the will of the Lord and being able to share the Gospel.'

'The call of God has its trials along the way,' Des confides. 'Despite the fact that we may have received an incredible call, confirmed by exciting prophetic words, we still have to work out our salvation on a daily basis and fulfil our ministry call. There will often be opposition against us when we set out to accomplish anything for the Lord, but we need to press on regardless – knowing that God will give us the grace to see us through.

'The Lord never asks us to do anything more than we can bear and He wants to fulfill all the dreams He has given us, despite the obstacles that may hinder us. His amazing grace is sufficient to take us from where we are right now to where we need to be!'

Chapter 18

Look Who is Cheering Us On

HEAVEN (PART 4)

Since we are surrounded by so great a cloud of witnesses... let us run with endurance the race that is set before us.

Hebrews 12:1

Given all he has been through, Des should not have survived many of his missionary trips to different countries – just as he should never have left Hamilton Hospital alive. But he had not completed his calling in God, and the Lord wasn't going to let His divine purposes and plans for Des and Ros miscarry.

Besides, they are not on their own. There has always been people praying for them on the earth and an even greater band of people rooting for them in heaven. What an encouragement, to have people supporting you both upstairs and downstairs!

Through Des's heavenly experience, he realized first-hand that he did not serve God alone, but that there was a long line of great men and women of the Bible whom the Lord had raised up, and each of these was an inspiration to him in their own way. For example, Moses.

When the Lord showed Des around his grandmother's mansion in heaven, he had seen something quite extraordinary. It was as if the embroideries in her home came alive with vivid pictures from the Bible.

There were images of angels and heavenly beings, and one with Moses standing at the shore of the Red Sea, striking the water with his staff. As Des examined one intricate embroidery, the colourful threads somehow seemed to change into a three-dimensional picture of the waves parting, and he could see the Israelites walking through a massive watery corridor to the other side.

'What an example of great faith and fearless obedience,' Des thought.

The embroidery was alive and had a story to tell, which was one of the most amazing things he had ever seen. All through heaven there seemed to be memorials like this to what God's people had accomplished.

Now the Lord was going to take Des to meet some of them, and He led Des back to the lake shore where there were a large number of people gathered. These were a part of the great cloud of witnesses that the Lord Jesus had told him about – the elders who, as Hebrews 11 puts it, obtained a good testimony and overcame many obstacles. *The Message* describes them as having accomplished the following:

> *Through acts of faith, they toppled kingdoms, made justice work, took the promises for themselves. They were protected from lions, fires, and sword thrusts, turned disadvantage to advantage, won battles, routed alien armies. Women received their loved ones back from the dead. There were those who, under torture, refused to give in and go free, preferring something better: resurrection. Others braved abuse and whips, and, yes, chains*

> *and dungeons. We have stories of those who were*
> *stoned, sawed in two, murdered in cold blood;*
> *stories of vagrants wandering the earth in animal*
> *skins, homeless, friendless, powerless – the world*
> *didn't deserve them!*
>
> Hebrews 11:32–38, *The Message*

Des looked at the crowd to see if he could recognize anyone, although as he saw their faces, he had an inner sense of knowing who the people were.

Then all at once, the prophet Elijah came walking towards them. Des knew who he was immediately. 'Elijah!' he exclaimed.

'Come walk with me,' the prophet invited.

Des began to share with Elijah how much he had been inspired through the Old Testament prophet's faith and obedience and all that he had accomplished for the Lord. 'You are one of the greatest prophets I've read about in the Bible,' he said. 'The Lord gave you such power and you called down fire from heaven...'

'Yes, I did, but listen to me, young man. Don't make the same mistakes as I made,' the prophet interjected. 'Yes, many great exploits were accomplished through my ministry, but there were also some very low periods. One minute I was calling down fire from heaven, and the next I was running for my life...

'My ministry was inconsistent, but the Lord was ever faithful, and He sustained me. Now learn from what I did wrong. There will be many times along your path when you will feel you are being tossed to and fro. There will be many occasions when you think that God is not with you, and men may reject you, and you will long to escape.

'But don't run, like me, and hide in a cave. Instead,

stand your ground and be focused on what God has told you to do. Even if you don't see things coming together for you, keep on walking and believing, because God will be with you – for that is the faith that the Lord will build your ministry upon.'

Des began to think about how Elisha had been discipled by this great man of God and how he had received a double portion of his anointing, and yet he had sometimes been mistreated by his master. 'What about Elisha?' he asked. 'You were quite harsh with the young prophet at times, when he was only trying to learn from you. Why did you treat him like that?'

'That was one of my weaknesses. I had little time for anybody but myself. I should have made more of an effort to impart more of what the Lord had given me to him. Don't be like that – take people with you wherever you go and invest all you have into them.

'Teach others, guide them and lift them up. Never be threatened by what God has called your disciples to do; rather, reproduce yourself in them. Build people up and don't expect them to run after you – build them up, and they will follow you,' Elijah concluded as their walk came to an end.

The Lord was still standing exactly where Des had left Him. 'There is another man I want you to meet,' He said, as Abraham came towards them.

'Come with me,' the ancient patriarch motioned to Des.

The young evangelist was delighted – this was the great 'father of many nations' whom God had cut covenant with, and raised up as the physical forefather of the Jewish people and the spiritual forefather of every believer in Christ.

'You have always inspired me as a great man of faith,' Des said. 'You left your father's house to pursue an unknown God and you followed Him into a far-off land. You had no idea what enemies would come against you or whether you would survive, but you had incredible faith and God was with you.'

'What you say is correct,' Abraham replied, 'and God will also take you into a foreign land. He will call you out of the land of your birth and take you into the wilderness, like me, to a sun-scorched place where water does not flow freely.

'It will be a hard land, a place which has come up against much opposition, where brother betrays brother and there is much bloodshed – a land that has destroyed itself and where darkness reigns. But God will lead you and you will put down roots. There will be much opposition against you, but be faithful, and just as I walked by faith and not by sight, go forward boldly. And as you do, so the Lord will keep His promises to you, as He kept His promises to me, and you and your descendants will be blessed.'

'My descendants?' Des asked. 'How many children am I going to have?'

'Your descendants will not be of the flesh, but of the spirit. They will be those whom you have brought to salvation; those whom you have imparted truth into and trained in ministry.

'And just as my descendants are as plentiful as the stars in the skies, so you too must call things that are not as though they were, and your descendants will be many through the preaching of the Gospel. God will bless you as you are faithful – now go!'

As Des turned back towards the crowd, the Lord Jesus approached with the Apostle Paul, one of the New Testament characters who had always inspired Des greatly.

'I love your writings! You were able to understand the words of the Lord and relate them to people in such a practical way,' Des said, 'and God used you so powerfully to establish so many churches.'

'Yes, and the Lord is going to use you in the same way!' the Apostle Paul exclaimed. 'On the road the Lord has called you to walk, you will plant many churches, just as I established many new works for the Kingdom.

'And God is going to give you the ability to lay hands on and appoint elders whom you will work alongside. You are going to build relationships with many churches all over the world, who will relate to you as a father figure, and you will travel backwards and forwards to minister to and encourage them.

'But one thing I want you to learn. Do not form a new denomination or network, where people are accountable to you financially. I never did that. I always worked with the churches I planted out of relationship, occasionally taking up an offering towards my work and to give to those in need.

'Do what God is calling you to do, in the same way as I did, and be content in all things, and you will be blessed by the Lord!'

The last great biblical figure who Des had the opportunity to converse with was one of Jesus' closest disciples, the Apostle Peter.

'This is Peter,' the Lord Jesus said. 'Walk with him a bit.'

Here was a man with a strong sense of purpose, who radiated life and enthusiasm – the disciple who had preached so powerfully on the day of Pentecost, bringing 3,000 people into the Church. 'What a great preacher he must be,' Des thought to himself.

'Yes, God gave me the ability to preach the Word,' Peter acknowledged, 'but I was filled with pride. Learn from me – don't allow your gift to make you think of yourself more highly than you ought. The moment I thought I was better than the other apostles was the moment the devil had a right to sift me like wheat' (see Luke 22:31–32).

'And that sifting shut the door of the Holy Spirit in my life, for a season. I felt the presence of the Lord leave me because of my arrogance. Do not allow that to happen to you. Rather, be like David, who was humble and cried out to God, pleading with Him that the Holy Spirit would never depart from his life – because without the presence of the Lord, we are nothing.

'The Lord has called you to be a preacher, as I was,' Peter said, 'but understand this: do not allow pride in your life, or seek the praises of men, because that will be the doorway to the devil's destruction of your life.'

This was a profound piece of advice and the last pearl of wisdom the great apostle offered, before the two men were back in the Lord's presence.

'The time has come for you to go back,' the Lord Jesus said to Des.

'But Lord, there is still much I must learn,' Des pleaded. 'This has been too short. I need to know more, so I don't make mistakes…'

'Get back in the boat!' the Lord replied. 'I have shown you things in part, but I will now show you them in full. As you keep close to me, so circumstances shall line up with your prayers, and all these things will be revealed to you in due course.'

'Thank you, Lord,' Des said, as a feeling of adoration radiated from his heart towards his beloved Saviour. 'I praise and worship You, for who You are and all You have done.'

As Des looked back towards the shore, he was encouraged by the sight of Elijah, Abraham, Peter, Paul and all the others standing on the edge of the lake.

'Do not worry!' they shouted. 'We are looking down upon you and we are cheering for you. You are not alone! Always remember – we have you surrounded!

'And never forget the things that we have spoken to you, because they will help you to accomplish all that the Lord has called you to do in the remaining time He has given you on earth.'

Chapter 19

Holding Out the Word of Life

LIFE EVANGELISM INTERNATIONAL

*Do everything without complaining or arguing, so
that you may become blameless and pure, children
of God without fault in a crooked and depraved
generation, in which you shine like stars in the
universe as you hold out the word of life.*

Philippians 2:14–16, NIV

Soul-winning and discipleship are two major facets in Des
and Ros Sinclair's ministry today, which fit together like a
hand in a glove. Without reaching out to people, there will
be no salvation, but without discipleship, salvation will be
short-lived.

Des and Ros have been prepared to sacrifice everything
for the cause of Christ – to see new converts come into
the Kingdom and to effectively disciple them so that they
too become fruitful and reproduce themselves in others.
Hopefully, through this book you have been encouraged
to become a more potent witness in the world you find
yourself in, and to become more available as a mentor for
other believers.

This is what the ministry of Life Evangelism is all
about – winning souls and empowering soul-winners. The
words of the prophet Elijah to Des during that heavenly

encounter continue to inspire him in ministry today to constantly be raising up a new generation of evangelists.

'Teach others, guide them and lift them up,' was the challenge he received then, 'and never be threatened by what God has called your disciples to do. Rather, reproduce yourself in them. Build people up and don't expect them to run after you – build them up, and they will follow you.'

For this reason, Des and Ros have committed themselves to walking closely with young trainee evangelists and upcoming ministers – not only teaching them all they have learnt from hard-earned experience, but taking them to the mission field as well.

One of Ros and Des's dreams is to convert a huge trailer into a potent evangelistic tool which provides accommodation for them and their trainee evangelists on the road, but which doubles up as a mobile platform for ministry, which can be used to hold crusades in outlying towns and villages.

In coming years, the Sinclairs hope to build a permanent missions base for Life Evangelism International (LEI) in South Africa, where they can accommodate, educate and disciple young, up-and-coming ministers of the Gospel. They also hope to build an orphanage for homeless or abandoned children.

Des and Ros have also formulated a unique evangelism training programme over their past ten years in Africa, to turn out a new generation of passionate young evangelists, helping them to gain practical experience in crusade preparation, in working with local churches and in the art of effective preaching. For the Sinclairs it is not about what they can do, but who God is raising up through them!

It is often said, 'You are not a success without a successor.' We as Christians have an awesome opportunity to impact others for the Kingdom, and what better legacy to leave behind than other believers whom we have mentored in the Lord. This is what the great commission is all about – making disciples of all nations – reproducing ourselves in others for the sake of the Kingdom.

May you be more open to learn from and share with fellow brothers and sisters in Christ, dear reader, so that Christ may be fully formed in you. And as you mature in the Lord, may He empower you not only to be a more effective soul-winner, but to raise up other soul-winners, for God has given each and every one of us the keys to setting people free.

> *Now thanks be to God who always leads us in triumph in Christ, and through us diffuses the fragrance of His knowledge in every place. For we are to God the fragrance of Christ among those who are being saved and among those who are perishing. To the one we are the aroma of death leading to death, and to the other the aroma of life leading to life.*
>
> 2 Corinthians 2:14–16 (NIV)

You too can spread the fragrance of the knowledge of Christ wherever you go, and as you do, God will give you victory in your life, helping you to overcome all fear, and go places you never thought possible. The world is in chains and we have been given the keys to unlock them.

'If people don't know Jesus, then they are prisoners to the devil, who rules their lives,' says Des. 'All men are prisoners in some area of their lives, and I can't bear to see people walking around in chains, because my God never created men and women to be bound, but to be free in Him.

'The devil chains people to their sin, but Jesus has come to loose the chains and set people free, and because I have been freed from my chains, I hold the key to unlock the chains of others through Jesus Christ. Everywhere I look, people are bound in chains, and yet, God has given all believers the key.'

The Lord once showed Des how He had placed a set of keys around his neck. 'Did I not go down to hell itself and take back the keys of life and death from the devil?' the Lord asked him. 'And have I not given you these keys to unlock those who are bound in chains? Now go and use them!'

'Lord, what is the key?' Des replied.

'The key is obedience to My Word, and knowing what you have been saved from must inspire and challenge you to unlock the chains of others.'

This book has recorded many examples of how Des and Ros have unlocked the chains of people, both physically and spiritually. Most recently, the Lord used Des mightily to address crime in the Western Cape region of South Africa. When Des visited Cape Town to speak at a conference, he was asked to help mediate between the gangs.

A high-ranking official was so impressed with Des's message that he asked him if he would consider meeting the gang leaders and see if he could talk some sense to them.

'These men were all drug-addicted murderers, possessed of the devil,' Des recalls, 'but I knew the Lord was opening up this opportunity, and so I was eager to go and share the power of the Gospel.'

Des told the gang leaders that God had seen their bondage and wanted to deliver them, and that if they repented from their sin, the Lord would unlock their chains and they would experience a freedom they had never known.

Then he began to minister in the word of knowledge, giving each of the men a specific personal prophecy.

Some of the gangsters started breaking down, and when Des gave a salvation call, all seven came forward, weeping.

'What you have said is correct,' one of the men said. 'Nobody could have known this, but God. Please help us.'

So Des led them in the sinner's prayer and began to cast out demons. Then he prayed against their drug addiction, asking God to fill them with the Holy Spirit. The Lord began to move in a powerful way. 'It was almost as if a wind was blowing in the room,' Des recalls, 'something which I have only seen once before, when we were ministering in Kenya.'

'We cannot go back to our gangs now,' one of the former gang leaders said. 'Please help us to disband them.'

'First we must put you into a drug rehabilitation programme,' one of the officials answered.

Two weeks later Des got a call from the rehab centre informing him that the seven men had come out of the rehab programme, and there were no signs of withdrawal symptoms or craving. God had supernaturally touched the men as a witness and a testimony to the whole community.

Des felt the Lord was leading him to tell the gang leaders to gather their members together at a nearby stadium. 'The power of God you have experienced is available to all,' he told the men. 'We need to share this with your gang members!'

Des and the organizers of the two-night evangelistic outreach were under no illusions as to what they were up against – a gathering of 25,000 hardened criminals in one place, where they could easily take each other on. It could become a blood-bath.

But the Lord had spoken, and Des was acting in faith. He was also encouraged by the fact that the Lord had told him to issue the gang leaders with a strong warning.

'Tell all your gang members to come,' he instructed the seven men, 'but make sure they don't bring any weapons with them, because God is declaring the stadium as holy ground, and if anyone comes in with a knife or gun, they will be struck down the moment they walk through the gate. Give everyone this important warning.'

Des has learnt that when the Lord speaks, one should take Him seriously. He knew the Lord wanted to deal with crime in a very serious way through this crusade meeting. In fact, not adhering to this simple warning was to prove to be a fatal mistake for a number of the gang members.

As two men walked through the stadium gate, they suddenly stopped breathing and collapsed. With a heavy security presence at the stadium, paramedics were called, but they could do nothing. The men had been carrying lethal blades and God had literally stopped them in their tracks.

Then another four men fell to the ground. They had been carrying powerful guns. In total six people died that night, sharing the same fate as Ananias and Sapphira, because they had defied the Lord (see Acts 5:5).

'Do not come in here with weapons!' Des shouted over the loudspeaker. 'Six men are dead because they came here carrying guns and knives – they are now being carried out on stretchers. You were warned – now I must caution you again. Leave your weapons at the gate, because if you walk in here with them, you will be struck down.'

It did not take long for a holy reverence to come upon the crowd, and many people who had not yet entered the stadium started dropping their weapons in front of the security checkpoint at the gate.

Over the two nights of the crusade, security personnel collected a whole van-load of guns, knives and all kinds of blades – the start of a disarming process that would bring peace and stability back into a troubled neighbourhood.

Encouraged by the amount of weapons being collected, Des started to preach in earnest. 'If you are responsible for killing your fellow man, God will hold you accountable for their blood.

'God's hand will be against you if you continue to commit such crimes, but if you repent, His grace is sufficient for you. Repent now, because you will one day have to give an account for all you have done. God has brought me here to reveal both His judgement and mercy to you. You are bound by the devil, but Jesus can set you free.'

This vast gathering of gangsters had seen God's presence in a way they could understand, and many gave their hearts to the Lord and experienced deliverance from drug addiction.

Through this one evangelistic outreach, reconciliation between gang members began to flow. Gangs were dispersed and many of the new converts began to work hand-in-hand with the police service, some of them speaking to school children and teenagers about the downward spiral that a life of crime would take them on, telling the students that they should rather live for God and fulfil all that He had called them to do with their lives.

'God is the only answer for crime,' Des says. 'Sinners do what sinners do because their consciences have been seared because of their blatant, ongoing sin, and only God can change their hearts. Only the Gospel has the power to change lives, as we reach out to more and more people and disciple them in the ways of the Lord.'

What an awesome privilege we have as believers,

living at this time in history. Des and Ros are continually amazed that the Lord has given each and every one of us such a powerful lifeline to throw out to others.

'It is such an honour to be called into the Kingdom in this hour and to be given the authority in the name of Jesus to help set men and women free,' says Des. 'Ros and I just want to do more and more for God, and use the keys He has given us to set people free, while we have still have breath. Our prayer is that God will continue to use us and help us to raise up others to impact the nations of the world.'

Chapter 20

You are Immortal Until God's Will for Your Life is Complete

CONCLUSION

'Everyday people, living the Book of Acts everyday!'

As you have read this book and seen the supernatural power of God at work to intervene in the lives of ordinary people, may you be encouraged to do more for God, literally putting your life on the line for Him, whatever it costs you, so that it becomes a lifeline for others. And all the time, looking fear in the face and defiantly rising up in faith – choosing not to trust in circumstances but in the Lord.

To accomplish our God-given call, we have to be sensitive to the Holy Spirit in our lives and overcome fear, because so many of us are rendered useless by fear of man, fear of the unknown, fear of death, fear of taking a risk – and the list goes on.

'I don't fear,' says Des, 'because I have nothing to be fearful about. If you are alive you can fear, but if you are dead, you can't. You cannot kill a dead man. That sums it up. I don't fear because my life is not mine, I have nothing to lose, everything that I had is lost and all that I am is Him.'

Ros and Des's advice to those who are held back by fear is to spend more time reading the Bible, which builds faith. As Romans 10:17 says: 'Faith comes by hearing the Word of God.'

'Overcoming fear boils down to obedience,' says Ros. 'It's that simple. I remember how challenging it was for me as a woman, going into prisons to minister with Des, but I had to put my love for the Lord first and be obedient to what He had called me to do. I had to look past myself and my comfort zones and step out of my complacency and do it for the Lord.

'And, by going into more and more prisons, I have gained tremendous confidence in God, and if anything, I find it really exciting seeing what God is doing in people's lives. I can now go anywhere, because I know the Lord is with me and I am there for His glory!'

Both Des and Ros Sinclair have stepped out and lived their dream. Who would have thought that a young boy whose education was so severely compromised, growing up on a rubbish dump, would today hold four university degrees?

Yet, God has taken this humble man, whom He personally taught to read His Word, and given him academic qualifications to match his remarkable life experience. Des currently has four degrees: A Bachelor of Divinity and a Master of Theology from Therapon University in the USA and a Doctorate of Divinity and a Doctorate of Ministry from Trinity University, also in the USA.

Ros has also received four professional qualifications: a diploma in Theology from Faith Bible College in New Zealand; a Bachelor of Divinity from Therapon University; a Master of Ministry and a Doctorate of Ministry from Trinity University. A gifted songwriter, she loves spending time alone with the Lord in praise and worship, and has written many worship songs.

One of Ros's most recent songs is entitled 'JAM Revolutionaries'. It gives believers an insight into what they can accomplish in partnership with the Lord. 'JAM' of course stands for 'Jesus and Me'!

JAM Revolutionaries

We are mighty soldiers,
In the army of the Lord.
We don't fight against flesh or blood,
But conquer demons with the sword.
We pray for others down on our knees,
And spread the Word by faith.
Mighty soldiers in Jesus,
Yeah – revolutionaries.

Chorus:
Soldiers in God's army,
And one of them is me.
We march towards the truth of light,
Defeating the enemy.
Jesus died and conquered hell,
And rose again – I know.
We stand for a new generation revolution,
Yeah – 'JAM' – Jesus and Me.

We march united side by side,
Together we are one.
Through the power of the blood,
We speak and proclaim the Son.
Darkness cannot stand us,
It bows and has to flee.
Through the mighty blood of Jesus,
We have the victory.

What the Lord has done for the Sinclairs, He will do similarly for you as you take on the mantle of a 'JAM revolutionary'. Whatever He has called you to do, though it may sound impossible, He will take to completion, because He is the God of the impossible.

While so many people give up because they are discouraged or fearful, JAM revolutionaries are a new breed of Christians who know they are immortal until the will of God is fulfilled in their lives, and no demon can stop them. They stand boldly in the full armour of God, overcoming every power and principality of darkness.

Will you become a JAM revolutionary today, with an inner conviction that Jesus and you are a majority? That as Jesus works through your life, you are His hands and His feet, and He will use you to touch the lives of all who you come into contact with?

This does not mean that your assignment from God won't take great faith and endurance on your part, but everything you do for Him is worth it because it has eternal value. You will invariably need to hang onto the promises of God with every fibre of your being, but, whatever you do, do not be derailed by the lies of the devil, who would try to keep you in fear for your life.

Will you make a decision today to put aside your everyday fears and put your life on the line for God so that it can become a lifeline for others? Will you stand alongside the other soldiers in the Lord's end time army, knowing that if God is for you, then no one can stand against you?

How do Des and Ros overcome stress and fear on a day-to-day basis?

'The greatest way to overcome fear is by confessing the Word of God,' says Des. 'As we seek the Lord through His Word and start stepping out in faith, that is when the

Holy Spirit will prompt and motivate us to go out and do something for God with great passion and confidence.

'This is why it is so important to be in the Word daily, surrounding ourselves with godly input through music, television and what we read. For example, watching Christian television is a wonderful opportunity to saturate yourself in the Word, as you receive the full counsel of God's Word from so many different preachers from across the world.

'Also, it's important to read and listen to the testimonies of others, including the writings of great men of God like Finney, Spurgeon and Moody. They were men of great passion who loved the presence of the Lord, and as a result of spending time in His presence, they were motivated to go out and do great exploits for Christ.

'Reading Christian autobiographies like these is so powerful because we defeat the devil by the blood of the Lamb and by the word of our testimony. Fellowship is also important, as we share our lives with others and encourage one another in the Lord.

'I am also greatly encouraged by the words of Isaiah, writing about the Messiah to come – that God will hold Him in His hand, and keep Him from harm. I know the prophet is referring to Jesus, and yet, through faith in Jesus Christ, the Lord has called each and every one of us in righteousness, and the same promise applies to us. And if the Lord will take hold of my hand and will keep me, then no devil, no man, no sickness, or any other thing can stand in the way of the Lord's hand holding me and keeping me for His glory.'

I, the Lord, have called You in righteousness,
and will hold Your hand; I will keep You and give

> *You as a covenant to the people, as a light to the*
> *Gentiles, to open blind eyes, to bring out prisoners*
> *from the prison, those who sit in darkness from*
> *the prison house.*
>
> Isaiah 42:6–7

The more we confess the Word of God on a daily basis and bask in His glorious presence, the more we will accomplish in God, the more breakthroughs will come as we move from glory to glory. Like David, who slew a bear and then a lion before he was ready to take on Goliath, as we begin to develop a series of smaller victories, so our faith will be built up to take on greater battles.

It may not happen overnight, but one day we will look back at the incredible testimony the Lord has given us because we were prepared to step out in obedience, fearless in our faith in God and simply trusting Him.

And remember how many times the words 'Fear not' appear in the Bible, perhaps most vividly in Isaiah:

> *Fear not, for I have redeemed you; I have called*
> *you by your name; You are Mine. When you*
> *pass through the waters, I will be with you; and*
> *through the rivers, they shall not overflow you.*
> *When you walk through the fire, you shall not be*
> *burned, nor shall the flame scorch you. For I am*
> *the Lord your God.*
>
> Isaiah 43:1–3

We as Christians today need to be so in tune with the voice of the Lord. God can speak to anyone, not only to those who pray for hours on end each day. Clearly, Des and Ros are in tune with the voice of the Holy Spirit, and you have read some of the amazing conversations Des has had in his head with the Lord.

The good news is that this level of intimacy is available to all believers. You too can learn to follow the voice of the Shepherd. As John 10:4–5 promises us, the sheep know their Master's voice and will not be misled by an impostor.

'The Lord can speak in many different ways,' says Ros, 'but I think primarily people must listen to their conscience, because that is His still, small voice in our hearts.'

'God has already spoken in His Word,' says Des. 'He has told us how we should live, but it is up to us to apply the principles that He has given us, by faith. And as we read the Scriptures, the Holy Spirit will convict us to fulfil the will of God for our lives and prompt us to action.

'Everything we hear that is in line with what the Bible teaches us, we should act upon in obedience. Obedience is the key thing. When God tells us to do something, we should go ahead and do it, even though we don't know how it is all going to work out at the time.

'By stepping out and acting upon what God has told you, that is when God intervenes and an anointing comes upon you. As Jesus said in what we call the great commission, "All authority has been given to Me – now go!" And that is what we should be doing today, pressing forward in His authority, because He has transferred it to us as believers.'

And Jesus came and spoke to them, saying, 'All authority has been given to Me in heaven and on earth. Go therefore and make disciples of all the nations, baptizing them in the name of the Father and of the Son and of the Holy Spirit, teaching them to observe all things that I have commanded

you; and lo, I am with you always, even to the end
of the age.'

Matthew 28:18–20

Jesus has given us His authority, through the finished work of the cross, but this will never be outworked if we don't obey the challenge to go. It is only as we step out in obedience that God's authority from heaven is manifest in our lives.

'This transfer of authority was not just for the twelve apostles but for the Church as a whole, as you can see by the example of the seventy in the Gospel of Luke. These were normal people, like you and I, who were carriers of God's power purely because they responded to the call,' Des says to encourage believers today.

After these things the Lord appointed seventy others
also, and sent them two by two before His face into
every city and place where He Himself was about
to go. Then He said to them, 'The harvest truly is
great, but the labourers are few; therefore pray the
Lord of the harvest to send out labourers into His
harvest.'

Luke 10:1–2

Be encouraged to step out in the name of Jesus, and proclaim His name and see the power of God flow through you, as experienced by the seventy. As Luke 10:17 says, 'Then the seventy returned with joy, saying, "Lord, even the demons are subject to us in Your name."'

Des and Ros believe that each and every believer needs such a paradigm shift in their thinking. These seventy people had previously seen the power of Jesus at work in

245

His ministry on the earth, but they were astounded when they discovered they could have the same power.

'They had seen demons bow their knee to Jesus, but did not believe that these evil spirits would bow to them in the name of Jesus,' says Des. 'But as they stepped out in obedience, so they began to realize that they were able to stand in the authority of Jesus.

'This power is available to all believers today, for in the name of Jesus there is power and authority, and we can cast out demons and lay hands on the sick and they will be healed. Yet some people are disobedient to the call because they are so afraid, because they have been listening to the lies of the devil.

'He is the greatest liar of all time, and he loves to keep Christians muzzled from sharing the Gospel, and will try anything to keep us from fulfilling our potential in God, by deceiving us with many different lies which instil fear in us or cause us to be preoccupied with ourselves.

'The devil doesn't have a big problem with us going to church and socializing, as long as we are not stepping out for God and reaching out to others. If all we are doing is talking about ourselves and how much God wants to bless and prosper us, we are no threat to him, neither will we be obedient to the call of God.

'But when we start asking ourselves the right questions, that is when we become a force to be reckoned with. Questions like: What does the Lord require of me? How can I be used to change a situation? And, how can I share my faith more effectively?

'God has put each and every one of us on this earth for a reason, for such a time as this (see Esther 4:14). He could have caused us to live at any time in history, but He chose to bring us into the world at this unique time, for His divine plans and purposes to be accomplished, and it is up to each and every one of us to find out what these are and fulfil them accordingly.'

How then, can they call on the one they have not believed in? And how can they believe in the one of whom they have not heard? And how can they hear without someone preaching to them? And how can they preach unless they are sent?

Romans 10:14–15, NIV

Will you follow in the footsteps of Des and Ros Sinclair? Will you be an ordinary person who is extraordinary for Jesus? Will you put your life on the line for God and become a lifeline for others?

Here is a prayer for you from Des and Ros:

Father, we pray for every reader of this book,
that as they have read about Your greatness,
and what You can do through simple lives,
they would be mightily encouraged
to step out in faith and do more for You.

And Lord, as they face difficult circumstances
and opposition in their everyday lives,
we pray that You would remind them of
the things Your Spirit has impressed
upon their hearts through this book.

We also pray that a spirit of boldness and
great courage would rise up within each reader,
and that they would trust You more fervently
to fulfil everything You have called them to do.
And we pray Your blessing upon every reader,
in the name of Jesus.
Amen.

Appendix 1

About Life Evangelism International

Life Evangelism International (LEI) is based in the city of Pretoria, South Africa, and is currently involved in the following projects:

Mass Gospel crusades
Preaching on television
Conference speaker
Business motivational speaker
Radio broadcasts
Prophetic ministry
Leadership development training
Training evangelists and ministers
Preaching in Bible seminaries
Preaching in schools
Short-term missions trips into Africa
Humanitarian aid through LEI Trust
Prison ministry
Hospital visitation ministry
Feeding homeless people
Preaching in churches (cross-denominationally)

Life Evangelism International contact details:

Des and Ros Sinclair
PO Box 4749
Rietvallei Rand
Pretoria 0174
South Africa

Telephone: +27 12 3451943
Mobile: +27 83 319 4627
Email: info@lei.org.za
Web: www.lei.org.za

Life Evangelism International Trust bank account details
(for donations to help with humanitarian and evangelism
work in Southern Africa):

ABSA Bank, Centurion Branch, Pretoria, South Africa
Account name: Life Evangelism International Trust
Account number: 405-492-8757
Branch sort code: 630-445
International Swift no.: ABSAZAJJ

APPENDIX 2

Ministry Endorsements

When Des and Ros Sinclair arrived in Nyeri, it was not long before the word began to spread like wildfire that a white man had come and that God had come with him, because all sorts of miracles were being performed in the name of the Lord. I personally testify to Des's credibility, as I have worked alongside him and have witnessed his devotion to God and unquenchable zeal. I have witnessed the blind receive new sight, the dumb talk, those with cancer healed, the demon-possessed freed, the barren conceive, and I have heard from reliable sources of the dead being raised.

Des and Ros came to Kenya in October 1998 and by January 1999, the territory of the enemy was uprooted and thrown out and the seed of the Kingdom of heaven was planted. His ministry has been a blessing that words cannot describe unless one experiences it. I trust that Des and Ros's ministry continues in the intensity and power of the Holy Spirit. Des never compromises the Word of God. He takes it literally for what God has said and I love him as a brother.

Pastor Zuli Osman Allu, Kenya

Evangelists Des and Ros Sinclair are a couple the Lord has used to make a significant impact in the lives of our congregation members and also across New Zealand. They have been known to me since 1993 but it was not until after their return from crusade ministries in Africa in 1999 that the Church in New Zealand really began to reap the fruit of their Holy Spirit giftings in preaching and miracle healings, coupled with an accurate prophetic Word of Knowledge that has caused many doubters to acknowledge the reality of God. Des and Ros have ministered in both small and large churches throughout New Zealand and everywhere they have been, many have accepted Christ into their lives. Our church has been immensely blessed by their ministry.

Dr Badu Bediako,
International Revival Church, New Zealand

Des Sinclair's prophetic ministry is both dynamic and uplifting. When he visited our church, he was 'right on' concerning many of the people he prophesied over. His preaching was also powerful because it was strongly based on the Word. Genuine healings also took place. For example, a father testified how his daughter's leg had grown four inches and was now the same length as her other leg. It was also obvious to me that Des and his wife, Ros, had no problem fitting in with a multicultural crowd. This to me, was a manifestation of their maturity and the compelling love of Christ in their hearts to share the Gospel regardless of cultural differences.

Pastor Tavale Matai'a,
Word of Life Church, Auckland, New Zealand

I have known Des and Ros for many years and have watched their ministry grow and develop. Des has a real gift in the area of Word of Knowledge and the prophetic anointing. He is able to bring the Word of God into a church and has a love to see the lost get saved, and while at Eden Assembly won many people to Christ. He has a genuine heart to see people get right with God and many backsliders have returned under his ministry. The other area where God has used this couple is that of healing. Again, I have seen first hand, people who were healed after prayer. The Sinclairs are a blessing to the body of Christ and always leave a spiritual deposit of souls which are saved, and people who are encouraged and healed.

Pastor Geoff Wiklund,
Eden Assembly of God, Auckland, New Zealand

I have had the privilege of knowing Des and Ros Sinclair personally for the past four years and have witnessed their faithfulness and dedication to their calling. During the period 1999 to 2003, I had the privilege of leading numerous teams of people to Malawi with the focus on practical and Word ministry. Des Sinclair accompanied us on one of these trips and my observation was that despite his exposure to some great exploits by God, he served our cause in humble capacities with distinction. This made an indelible impression on the other members and I, who were all volunteer businessmen. Due to the specific focus on evangelism to the poor and those in remote and hostile areas, the road the Sinclairs travel on is more often than not, a lonely one. However their availability to pour out their lives as an offering to the Lord Jesus Christ, has been exemplary and an inspiration to many.

Raymond Fuchs,
Businessman, South Africa